Cooking With Annie D

Southern Recipes Seasoned With Seagraves and Pettyjohn Family History

Donny Bailey Seagraves

COILE GROVE
PRESS

Published by
COILE GROVE PRESS
Athens, Georgia

Published by Coile Grove Press, Athens, GA

ISBN: 978-1-958713-00-6

First Edition 2022
10 9 8 7 6 5 4 3

Cover art by Jodie Locklear

Unless otherwise noted, all photos are from Anne "Annie D" Pettyjohn Seagraves' photo albums or Phillip and Donny Bailey Seagraves' photo albums.

Epigraph

"Pull up a chair. Take a taste. Come join us. Life is so endlessly delicious."—Ruth Reichl

Contents

Cooking With Annie D

Southern Recipes Seasoned With Seagraves and Pettyjohn Family History

Dedication

This book is dedicated to current and future members of the Seagraves and Pettyjohn families. By learning more about those who came before you — who they were, where they lived, what they cooked — I hope you will come to know more about yourselves. I also hope you will continue our traditions of cooking Southern food and that you will add more good chapters to our Seagraves and Pettyjohn family histories.
—Donny Bailey Seagraves, July 31, 2022, Athens, Georgia

Acknowledgments

Many thanks go out to Hope Seagraves Austin, Rebecca Seagraves Baugh, Todd Burroughs, Judith Coile Donohoe, Mary Seagraves Fields, Suzanne Seagraves Gerling, Carol Pettyjohn Hitt, Missy Seagraves Jackson, Tristin Seagraves Johnson, Gail Langer Karwoski, Bessie Seagraves Kemp, Jodie Locklear, Lori Fields Loden, Pati Tiller Montgomery, Marcia Fair Norris, Steve Norris, Luke Pettyjohn, Mabel Farr Pettyjohn, Rev. Gene Pettyjohn, Wayne Pettyjohn, Miriam Rushton, Ann Shellnut Seagraves, Billy Seagraves, Freddy Seagraves, Jen Seagraves, John Seagraves, Phillip Seagraves, Sandy Seagraves, Terrie Wages Seagraves, Todd Seagraves, Bill Simmons, Kay Thomas, Carla Wade, Myra C. Manley Watkins Walker and Margie Strickland Ward, for information, memories, pictures, recipes, editing, proofreading and more. Some of you contributed a lot, some a little, but you all helped make this book possible. I'm forever grateful.

Introduction

Her full name was Exa Annie Derrell Pettyjohn Seagraves. But we just called her Annie D, Anne, mother, grandmother, sister, aunt, cousin, mother-in-law, or friend. She talked in a twangy mountain accent acquired while growing up in the North Georgia towns of Lafayette and Dalton.

In 1933, after moving as a teenager to Athens, Georgia, along with her parents, William "Will" and Ethel Strickland Pettyjohn, and four of her six siblings, Willie Belle, Vic, Luke, and Mary, Anne found another town to love.

Other than her husband, native Athenian Nelson Hardy "Petie" Seagraves, Anne's obsessions were her three children: William Harvey "Billy" Seagraves, Mary Ethelyn Seagraves Fields, and Phillip Nelson Seagraves, plus her seven grandchildren: Suzanne Seagraves Gerling, Sandy Seagraves, Lori Fields Loden, Kevin Fields, Travis Fields, Jen Seagraves, and Greg Seagraves.

A young Anne "Annie D" Pettyjohn Seagraves standing near City Hall in downtown Athens, Georgia

Anne also loved fishing in area lakes and cooking in her cozy Eastside Athens, Georgia kitchen in the house on Georgia Drive, near the University of Georgia's Sanford Stadium.

Reception Salad {Aunt Agnes's way}

1 box lemon jello
2/3 cup {chopped} celery
2/3 cup {chopped} nuts
1/2 pint whipping cream
1 #1 can crushed pineapple
1-8 oz cream cheese
1/2 teaspoon salt

Drain juice from pineapple & heat and dissolve jello into hot juice. Let thicken and add other ingredients. Have cream cheese softened and cream whipped before adding to jello mixture

Annie D's handwritten reception salad (Aunt Agnes' way) recipe

Lucky for us, before Anne gradually lost her memory to Alzheimer's, she wrote down some of her favorite recipes, photocopied them, and put them in binders for her children and grandchildren. This book contains many of those cherished recipes, along with others found tucked into her favorite cookbooks.

Also included are recipes from Anne's family members, neighbors, and others, plus several recipes from another Ann Seagraves of the Madison County branch of the Seagraves family.

Some of our favorite foods, such as Anne's fried chicken and sweet potato pie, are missing from this book. She made those Southern favorites throughout her adult life without using recipes. She probably thought we would know how to make them, too. Most of us sorta do, though our versions will never be the same as Anne's.

Athens Mayor Jack R. Wells and First Ward Councilmember Harvey Lee "Bob" Seagraves view a public works project on East Broad Street, circa 1949.—Photo by former Athens City Engineer Walter Beacham

The recipes in this book are seasoned with Seagraves and Pettyjohn family history, plus memories and family photos. You will read about how our Seagraves ancestors moved from North Carolina to Madison County, Georgia, early in the county's history and then how some Seagraves, including fraternal twins Hardy and Andy, left the farm and moved to the town of Athens in the 1860s.

Hardy's son Harvey Lee "Bob" Seagraves represented the City of Athens First Ward as a council member for 25 years. His older brother Charles E. "Hard Charlie" Seagraves, was a well-known Athens police chief. Another brother, Fred "Shack" Seagraves, worked as a police captain and chief of detectives. You'll read about them and their other siblings, including Edward Pope "Fid" Seagraves, who became one of the most successful farmers and business owners in Clarke County.

Several restaurants were founded and operated by Seagraves descendants, including Mark Ed Hansford and Susan DeRose. You'll read about these, and you'll learn about the history of Madison County's historic Seagraves Mill. This once-thriving business was purchased and operated by Josiah Milsey Seagraves in the early 1900s.

L-R: Mabel Farr Pettyjohn, Luther "Luke" Pettyjohn and Rev. Eugene "Gene" Pettyjohn at Annie D and Petie Seagraves' 50th wedding anniversary party in the basement of Oconee Street Methodist Church

Anne Seagraves' maiden name was Pettyjohn. In these pages, you will find a well-researched and lovingly written family history article by Anne's late brother and sister-in-law, Luke and Mabel Pettyjohn. In Luke and Mabel's article, you'll meet Pettyjohn and related family ancestors, including those who once lived on Pigeon Mountain in North Georgia, near Lafayette, Georgia. This land today is part of a 20,657-acre state-owned Wildlife Management Area in Northwest Georgia that features abundant wildlife, miles of trails, unique natural features, and gorgeous mountain views.

Pettyjohn kitchen cabinet from the house on Boulevard. To the right, is the charcoal portrait of Jacob and Sarah Bankston Pettyjohn.—Photo by Donny Bailey Seagraves

You'll read about Jacob Pettyjohn and his wife, Sarah Bankston Pettyjohn, who once posed for a traveling artist. Their charcoal portrait today hangs in a descendant's dining room, near Ethel Pettyjohn's beloved art déco Hoosier kitchen cabinet from her kitchen in the Pettyjohn house on Boulevard in downtown Athens, Georgia. You'll also read profiles of Will and Ethel Pettyjohn's seven children.

We wish we had more Annie D recipes and more Seagraves and Pettyjohn family history to share. At the same time, we're thankful to have the recipes Anne and others left for us and the family history, photos, and other information we have shared on these pages. Our memories of Annie D's Georgia Drive kitchen and her love are delicious, too, and continue to nourish and feed us all.—*Donny Bailey Seagraves, Annie D's daughter-in-law and a Seagraves family member since 1970.*

Chapter 1

Welcome to the Seagraves Family

Mom invited us for lunch tomorrow, my future husband Phillip Seagraves said one day, not long after we started dating.

I had met Phillip's parents a few weeks earlier and looked forward to getting to know them better and seeing the Seagraves' house.

Phillip and I had known each other vaguely in school when we were in the same math class at Pattie Hilsman Junior High the first year that school (now called Hilsman Middle School) opened.

After our year at Hilsman, we attended Athens High School but didn't have any classes together. The next time Phillip and I encountered each other was one day when I rode home from school with my dad, and he steered our car into the Pete Seagraves Service Station drive on Oconee Street and pulled up by a gas pump.

In those days, the word "service" in service station meant someone came out and pumped your gas for you. While gas filled your tank, the service station attendant washed your car's windshield.

On that day, the person who pumped our gas and washed our

windshield was Phillip Seagraves. I recognized him from our long-ago math class, but he had certainly changed. He looked taller and slimmer as he beamed a smile at me through the sparklingly clean windshield. I couldn't help but smile back.

The Bailey family 1956 T-bird. At the time this book was written, this car was still in the family.—Photo by Donny Bailey Seagraves

After graduating from high school, I entered the University of Georgia as a journalism major. I didn't see Phillip again until one Sunday when my dad, who, along with Phillip and several other men, had founded the Athens Antique Auto Club, asked if I would go to the meeting and drive our 1956 T-bird.

I drove the aqua T-bird that day with my younger brother Mike as a passenger. As fate would have it, the gorgeous but mechanically challenged car broke down.

Phillip Seagraves with his 1939 Hudson

Mike and I were wondering what to do when along came Phillip in his 1939 Hudson.

"Need a ride?" he asked.

"Sure," I said.

Phillip was funny and cute that day. Next thing I knew, we were dating.

The Seagraves house at 215 Georgia Drive

215 Georgia Drive

The day of our lunch with Phillip's parents was my introduction to the Seagraves house at 215 Georgia Drive.

"Something smells delicious," I said as Phillip and I made our way through the living room furnished with comfortable-looking furniture into the kitchen at the back of the house. Anne stood at the stove, frying something golden brown in a black iron skillet.

Nearby, Pete sat at the square oak table, drinking sweet iced tea and playing solitaire. He was heavier then and sported a buzz cut that showed off his prominent widow's peak.

Anne looked trim and comfortable in her baggy shirt and oversized apron. We greeted each other. Then she turned back to the stove to finish cooking the rest of our lunch.

When it was done, Anne set a steaming platter of Southern fried chicken in front of me.

"Help yourself," she said.

Nelson Hardy "Petie" Seagraves in the Georgia Drive house kitchen

I selected a piece, then filled my plate with sides and a biscuit. After Anne, Pete and Phillip got their food, we all dug in.

The fried meat tasted like chicken — but not quite, I thought after my first bite. Regardless of what part of the chicken it was, it tasted delicious. I finished that piece, then reached for another, which turned out to be a rabbit's foot.

Annie D Seagraves in her Georgia Drive house kitchen

A rabbit's foot! I had never eaten rabbit before, even though I came from pioneer Georgia families on both sides. The Baileys from Wilkes County and the Coiles from Oglethorpe County must have killed and eaten many rabbits and other game to survive when they cleared the land and built their farmhouses several generations ago. But I'd never eaten rabbit. I guess I was a city girl, even though I lived in rural Winterville, where cottontails far outnumbered people.

That long-ago rabbit lunch was my initiation into the Seagraves family. It also was the first of many out-of-this-world delicious Southern meals, animated conversations, and penny poker games in the homey, high-ceilinged Georgia Drive kitchen with Anne and Pete and numerous extended family members over a span of almost 30 years.

And it was the first and last time I ever ate rabbit.—*Donny Bailey Seagraves, daughter-in-law of Annie D*

Donny Bailey Seagraves and Phillip Nelson Seagraves in 1970

Chapter 2

Appetizers

Origins of the Segraves/Seagraves Surname

Seagraves is a famous English surname. Many of us have always thought that the sea in Seagraves refers to the literal sea, but according to research, our last name may have nothing to do with the sea.

Instead, the name is considered locational, from a village called Seagrave, in Leicestershire, the very center of England. During the Middle Ages, many people migrated to find a job and often took the name of their former village for identification.[1]

Another Possible Origin of the Segraves/Seagraves Surname

In the work of Professor D. D. Stokes, *Ireland and the Celtic Church,* he states that the name Seagraves is Danish. In many Irish scholarly works, the family name is referred to as being Danish . . . From the first time the wives of the de Segrave men were recorded until the last traceable European Segrave, they married almost exclusively women from prominent Norman families. Even in Ireland, they married only a handful of Irish women in 600 years. So, in a sense, the Segrave/Seagraves heritage might be more Norman than anything else.[2]

Coat of Arms

Seagraves

Historiography

The Seagraves Coat of Arms illustrated left was drawn by an heraldic artist from information officially recorded in ancient heraldic archives. Documentation for the Seagraves Coat of Arms design can be found in Burke's General Armory. Heraldic artists of old developed their own unique language to describe an individual Coat of Arms. In their language, the Arms (shield) is as follows:

"Sa. a lion ramp. ar. ducally crowned or."

When translated the Arms description is:

"Black, a silver lion attacking, wearing a gold ducal crown."

Above the shield and helmet is the Crest which is described as:

"Six arrows fretwise and three paleways, points downwards all ppr. all interlaced and bound together with a wreath of the colors."

A translation of the Crest description is:

"Six arrows woven and three vertically, points downwards all natural; all interlaced and bound together with a wreath of the colors."

Family mottos are believed to have originated as battle cries in medieval times. A Motto was not recorded with the Seagraves Coat of Arms.

Individual surnames originated for the purpose of more specific identification. The four primary sources for second names were: occupation, location, father's name and personal characteristics. The surname Seagraves appears to be locational in origin, and is believed to be associated with the English, meaning, "one who came from, or lived near Seagrave (lake grove)." The supplementary sheet included with this report is designed to give you more information to further your understanding of the origin of names. Different spellings of the same original surname are a common occurrence. Dictionaries of surnames indicate probable spelling variations. The most prominent variations of Seagraves are Seagrave, Seagrove, Seagroves and Seagraven.

Census records available disclose the fact there are approximately 600 heads of households in the United States with the old and distinguished Seagraves name. The United States Census Bureau estimates there are approximately 3.2 persons per household in America today which yields an approximate total of 1920 people in the United States carrying the Seagraves name. Although the figure seems relatively low, it does not signify the many important contributions that individuals bearing the Seagrave name have made to history.

No genealogical representation is intended or implied by this report and it does not represent individual lineage or your family tree.

HALBERTS 3687 Ira Road - Bath, Ohio 44210

©Halberts

A Seagraves Family Coat of Arms—From Freddy Seagraves

Seagraves in America

Most Seagraves are probably related to the original de Segrave family that was first recorded in the Domesday Book and to people who once lived in the hamlet of Seagraves in Leicestershire.

However, according to the website: theseagravesfamilyinameri ca.com, no specific links have yet been verified between the American and the European branches of the Seagraves family. We do know from records found during research that most Seagraves families in America derive from three initial settlements:

- Massachusetts Settlement
- New Jersey Settlement
- North Carolina Settlement

Most, if not all, of the Seagraves family members you will read about in this book descend from the North Carolina Settlement.[3]

~

Anne "Annie D" Seagraves holding daughter Mary Seagraves Fields; Nelson "Petie" Seagraves with oldest son Billy Seagraves. Youngest son Phillip Seagraves had not yet been born.

Cheese Straws

- *1/2 pound cheese, grated*
- *Cayenne pepper*
- *1 1/2 cups flour*
- *1/2 cup butter*
- *Pinch of salt*

Mix the above ingredients and then mix with flour. Roll and cut into straws. Bake at 375 degrees until done.—*Anne Seagraves, Clarke County, Georgia*

L-R: Billy Seagraves, Mary Seagraves Fields, and their uncle David Seagraves, who is the youngest son of Harvey Lee "Bob" and Reba Seagraves, in front of a house at the corner of Little Oconee and South Poplar Streets. Pete and Annie D and their two older children Billy and Mary lived in this house before they bought the house at 215 Georgia Depot Street (later called Georgia Drive).

Cranberry Cheese Ball

- *2 bags of shredded cheddar cheese (8 ounces each, mild or sharp. Leave packages of shredded cheese out of refrigerator to soften).*
- *8 ounces dried cranberries*
- *8 ounces chopped nuts (pecans or walnuts)*
- *3 tablespoons orange juice*
- *1/3 cup white sugar*

In a large mixing bowl, blend all ingredients, form into a ball, and then refrigerate overnight.—*Ann Seagraves, Madison County, Georgia*

Phillip Seagraves in Annie D's Georgia Drive house kitchen, in the late 1950s

Crabmeat Dip

- *1 package frozen crabmeat (6-ounce package, thawed and drained)*
- *1/2 cup mayonnaise*
- *1/4 cup milk (sweet)*[4]
- *1 package cream cheese (8 ounces, softened)*
- *Dash of onion salt*

Shred crab meat. Combine mayonnaise, milk, cream cheese, and onion salt. Blend until smooth. Stir in crabmeat. Spoon into 1-quart casserole. Bake uncovered at 350 degrees for 20 minutes. Yields 2 ½ cups.—*Anne Seagraves, Clarke County, Georgia*

Taco Dip

- *1 package Philadelphia Cream Cheese (8 ounces, softened)*
- *1 can Hormel Chili without beans (15 ounces)*
- *1 small jar of chopped olives (5-6 ounces)*
- *1/2 pound shredded Colby cheese*
- *1/2 pound shredded sharp cheddar cheese*

Spread cream cheese on greased pie plate, then layer other ingredients in order. Bake uncovered at 350 degrees until bubbly (about 15 minutes). Serve with chips.—*Ann Seagraves, Madison County, Georgia*

Date Fingers

- *1 ½ sticks margarine*
- *2 cups sugar*
- *2 beaten eggs*
- *½ pound package chopped dates*
- *1 1/3 cups Rice Krispies*
- *1 cup chopped nuts*
- *2 teaspoons vanilla*
- *1 box finely grated coconut*

Melt margarine. Add eggs, sugar, and dates. Cook 10 minutes on low heat. After the mixture comes to a boil, keep stirring so dates won't stick. Remove from heat and add vanilla, nuts, and Rice Krispies. When cool, make rolls the size of finger and roll in coconut.—*Anne Seagraves, Clarke County, Georgia*

Nippy Deviled Eggs

- *8 hard-boiled eggs*
- *1/4 cup mayonnaise*
- *1 teaspoon prepared mustard*
- *1/2 to 1 teaspoon of prepared horseradish*
- *1/4 teaspoon salt*
- *1/4 teaspoon pepper*
- *1/4 teaspoon paprika*

Cut eggs in half lengthwise and remove yolks. Mash yolks. Stir in mayonnaise, mustard, horseradish, salt, and pepper. Fill egg halves with mixture. Chill and sprinkle with paprika before serving.—*Anne Seagraves, Clarke County, Georgia*

Chapter 3

Early Seagraves Family History

This early Seagraves family history information is from a book entitled *Segraves/Seagraves and Related Families of Northeast Georgia* by Myra C. Manley Watkins Walker. Myra's grandfather was George T. Seagraves, Sr.

Myra's book, self-published in 1993, may be out of print, but you might find a copy in the Madison County, Georgia, library or other area libraries. You may also find a used copy online on sites such as https://used.addall.com. Hopefully, the author will republish this book in the future. Many thanks to Myra for allowing us to include this excerpt about our branch of the Segraves/Seagraves family here.

John Segraves

John Segraves, who lived in Madison County, Georgia, between 1821 and 1828, may have been the same John Segraves who lived in Anson County, North Carolina, between 1800 and 1820. A William Segraves also lived in Anson County during this time.

John Segraves of Madison County married Martha (maiden name unknown). She was nicknamed Patsy and was born between

1750 and 1760. According to an Anson County, North Carolina 1810 census report and other records, John and Patsy may have been the parents of two daughters born between 1775 and 1784, William, Burrell, a son born between 1790 and 1800, and Parthena, born about 1805.

John Segraves of Adair's district in Madison County drew in the 1827 land lottery. By July 7, 1828, he had died because records show that on that date, James Anderson and Whitmire H. Adair applied for letters of administration on the estate of John Segraves, deceased. Widow Segraves and William Segraves bought property from the sale of the personal estate of John Segraves.

Patsy appeared in the 1830 Madison County Census report. Also living in her household was a female between twenty and thirty years old. This may have been Parthena, who appeared on the 1850 Madison County, Georgia Census, age 45, living alone.

Patsy Segraves drew in the land lottery and gold lottery of Madison County, as did William Segraves. She was listed as Martha Segraves, widow living in Sea's district. On May 2, 1836, Whitmire H. Adair, administrator for John Segraves' estate, sold one hundred and thirty-six acres of land to James Anderson. Most likely, Patsy had died shortly before this time. No other records have been located on her.

William Issac Buchner (Buck) Segraves

William "Buck" Segraves may have been the son of John and Martha "Patsy" Segraves. According to family legend, he married Cheney, whose maiden name was Strickland. Cheney was born in North Carolina about 1791.

According to land deed records, Buck and Cheney came to Madison County in 1821. With them came several small children and John and Patsy. Buck paid one hundred dollars to John Pittman for one hundred and eleven acres of land on the banks of Sandy Creek.

Buck and Cheney appeared in the 1830 Madison County, Georgia Census. Their household included three males under the age of five, three between the ages of five and ten, two between the ages of fifteen and twenty, and one between the age of forty and fifty. There were only two females; one between the age of ten and fifteen and the other between thirty and forty.

Buck and Cheney also were listed on the 1840 and 1850 Madison County census records. According to Union Baptist Church records, Cheney died on December 18, 1852. She may have died of typhoid fever since four members, according to family legend, died of the fever in the early 1850s. Buck died after Cheney, but the exact date is not known. According to family legend, they are buried in a field near Seagraves Mill.

Buck and Cheney were parents of at least eleven children. Family legend says twelve — ten boys and two girls. It is possible another sister existed and died before coming to Georgia or that she was Sarah Bridges, but this is unknown.

The children of Buck and Cheney were:

Noah Segraves
Elizabeth Segraves
Alfred Segraves
William Segraves, Jr.
Clem Segraves
Milsey Segraves
Hardy Segraves
Burgess (Birdy) Segraves
James Calloway (Callie), Segraves
Sampson Segraves
Zachariah Lumpkin Segraves.

At some point, Noah changed the spelling of his last name from Segraves to Seagraves.

Noah Seagraves

Noah Seagraves probably was the oldest child of William and Cheney. He was born in North Carolina about 1807 and died probably in 1852, for family legend says he died of typhoid fever. He married Rebecca Williams in Madison County, Georgia, on April 3, 1833.

Rebecca Williams Seagraves was born in 1811 to Robert and Frances Flanagan Williams. Robert Williams, Sr. and his wife had nine children. Rebecca died in 1881. She is thought to be buried in the Williams-Smith/Baugh/Boggs cemetery. Noah is believed to be buried in the Seagraves family cemetery on Mr. Adams' land near Neese.

The children of Noah and Rebecca were:

Lucinda Seagraves Bridges
Mary Ann Seagraves Blair
William Seagraves
Josiah Milsey Seagraves
Hardy Calloway Seagraves
Andrew Mathew Seagraves

Many more Segraves/Seagraves family members are included in Myra C. Manley Watkins Walker's book, Segraves/Seagraves and Related Families of Northeast Georgia. Most of the Seagraves in Cooking With Annie D descend from Noah and Rebecca Williams Seagraves' children: Hardy, Andrew, William, and Josiah Milsey Seagraves.—Donny Bailey Seagraves[1]

Chapter 4

Hardy Seagraves: From Madison County to Athens, Georgia

Driving through the picturesque countryside of Madison County, Georgia, husband Phillip and I often wondered why Phillip's paternal great-grandfather, Hardy Calloway Seagraves, moved away from this rural area over 150 years ago.

Hardy and his fraternal twin brother Andrew Mathew "Andy" Seagraves were born July 6, 1851, on a Madison County family farm. In those days, forty percent of babies died before their fifth birthday; twin mortality rates were even higher. But somehow, despite those brutal odds, the Seagraves twins survived.[1]

Hardy and Andy were the youngest children of Noah and Rebecca Williams Seagraves. Older siblings included Lucinda Elizabeth, born October 9, 1835; William Robert, born about 1842; Mary Ann, born November 7, 1845; and Josiah Milsey, born January 27, 1846.

Hardy's father, Noah, migrated from Cribb's Creek, Anson County, North Carolina, to Madison County, Georgia, with his parents, William Issac "Buck" Segraves and Priscilla Cheney Strickland Segraves, and other family members, in 1821. By 1833, Noah was listed on the Georgia Property Tax Digest in the Nowhere District of Madison County, Georgia, as was his father, William Isaac "Buck" Segraves. The latter was probably a son of John Segraves.[2]

Segraves/Seagraves

Family Tree

John Segraves & Martha "Patsy" (maiden name unknown) Segraves

|

William Issac Buchner "Buck" Segraves & Cheney Strickland Segraves

|

Noah Seagraves & Rebecca Williams Seagraves

|

Hardy Calloway Seagraves & fraternal twin brother Andrew Mathew "Andy" Seagraves, older brothers William Seagraves and Josiah Milsey Seagraves, older sisters Lucinda Seagraves Bridges and Mary Ann Seagraves Blair

According to family legend and records of the Union Baptist Church of Madison County, Georgia, Noah most likely died in 1852, along with his father Buck, mother Cheney, and possibly one other family member, of typhoid fever.

Typhoid Fever was a common cause of death in the 1800s, especially in rural areas such as Madison County, Georgia. There were no antibiotics to treat this illness at the time, which is characterized by a persistently high fever, rash, generalized pains, headache, and severe abdominal discomfort.

Hardy and Andy were only about two years old when their father, grandparents, and possibly another family member passed away. The toddler twins would have had no memories of these Madison County pioneer settler family members. Hopefully, they heard many stories about them from their mother and older brothers and sisters.[3]

The Civil War

When the Civil War began on April 12, 1861, Hardy and Andy were almost ten years old, too young to volunteer or be conscripted. Both of their older brothers fought for the Confederate army.

William married Nancy Sailors in Madison County, Georgia, on January 23, 1862. He enlisted in White's Company and fought as a private in the Georgia Infantry. He returned home after the war and lived in Athens, Clarke County, with his wife and children.

Double-barreled cannon in front of Athens, Georgia City Hall—Photo by Donny Bailey Seagraves

William, whose descendants include Joseph Seagraves, born about 1864, Thomas Seagraves, born about 1867, Andrew Seagraves, born about 1869, Mammie Seagraves, born about 1873 and William Seagraves, Jr., born about 1877, died in Clarke County in 1880. Some of his Seagraves descendants once lived on land that includes Seagraves Drive, off Lexington Road, and may still live in the Athens area today.

Weyman Seagraves, Josiah Milsey Seagraves' grandson—From Tristin Seagraves Johnson

Josiah married Clarisa "Clara" A. Riden on June 9, 1867, in Athens, Clarke County. According to Clara's widow's pension application filed in 1922, Josiah enlisted September 1863 in the Adams Battalion, Company A, in Athens, Georgia, at age seventeen.

Josiah Milsey Seagraves used this gun, a cap and ball double-barreled shotgun, when he served in the Confederate Army during the Civil War.—From John Seagraves

---

> "My great-grandfather, Josiah Milsey Seagraves, guarded a bridge over the Oconee River in Athens, Georgia, during the Civil War. His gun from the Civil War has been passed down in our family. It's a cap and ball double-barreled shotgun. Most militia members furnished their own guns as they prepared for Sherman's raids after the Battle of Atlanta."
>
> — John Seagraves

Josiah returned home after the war and lived in Athens. He was listed on a Georgia U.S. Property Tax Digest for Clarke County in 1890. He then lived in District 217, also known as the Athens Factory District.

At some point, Josiah moved to Jackson County and then back

to Madison County, where he purchased an almost 100-year-old gristmill in 1906 and renamed it Seagraves Mill.

A closeup view of the cap and ball double-barreled shotgun Josiah Milsey Seagraves used during the Civil War—From John Seagraves

His descendants include Lee Seagraves, born March 7, 1868, Alice N. Seagraves, born March 11, 1870, Dora Seagraves, born April 11, 1873, Alcie Seagraves, born December 1, 1874, Mollie Seagraves, born November 20, 1877, Veonie Seagraves, born November 5, 1880, Lonie C. D. Milsey Seagraves, Sr., born October 24, 1882, Naomi Seagraves, born June 26, 1885, Carl Calvin Seagraves, born January 26, 1889, Arthur Ford Seagraves, born July 22, 1892, and Bessie Seagraves, born August 8, 1897.

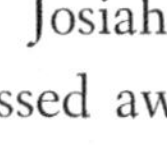

Josiah passed away in Madison County in 1917 and is buried in the Gordon's Chapel United Methodist Church Cemetery in Hull, Georgia. Some of his descendants still live in Madison County today.[4]

Josiah Milsey Seagraves' grave in Madison County, Georgia—From Tristin Seagraves Johnson

Leaving Madison County

Sometime between 1860, when Hardy is listed in the Madison County census record as a nine-year-old son of Rebecca Seagraves, farmer, and 1870, when Hardy, age eighteen, is recorded as a cotton mill worker, son of Rebecca Seagraves who is keeping house in Athens, Clarke County, Hardy, Andy, older sister Mary Ann and their mother traveled the rutted dirt roads by wagon from their Madison County farm to Athens. They settled in the Eastern part of the small but growing town of about 4,000 people. Other family members may have come with them or moved to Athens at a different time.[5]

American artist George Cooke's painting, View of Athens from Carr's Hill, though painted in 1845, shows a scene similar to what Hardy, Andy and other family members would have seen when they arrived from Madison County. During this time, the railroad tracks ended at Carr's Hill, the area where Anne "Annie D" and Nelson "Petie" Seagraves later lived on Georgia Drive (originally Georgia Depot Street). This view today would be near Oak Street, before crossing the Oconee River. Downtown Athens and the University of Georgia are visible in the background.—Courtesy of Hargrett Rare Book and Manuscript Library/University of Georgia Libraries

Athens, Georgia in the 1860s

When the Seagraves family moved to Athens, they had probably only traveled about twenty miles from their rural Madison County farm. It might have taken them most of the day by horse and wagon to reach their destination. Today, the same trip by car would only take about thirty minutes, depending on your route and how fast you drove.

Carr's Hill ancient rock wall that surrounds the Eastside Athens, Georgia property—Photo by Phillip Seagraves

Though it was not too far from Madison County, Athens in the 1860s must have seemed like a whole different world to young Hardy and Andy. They may have approached Athens on the East side, in the Carr's Hill area, where they would have traveled past the stone wall surrounding the Carr property. This wall, initially begun in 1789 by Elijah Walker, was completed in 1831-1832 by William A. Carr to protect his family from harm. The ancient stone wall was still standing on Carr's Hill when this book was written.[6]

Much of East Athens would have been a dense forest of pine and cedar as the Seagraves traveled past Carr's Hill to the Oconee River. The twins would have seen abundant wild game, including flocks of turkeys and coveys of quail. There were cotton fields, too, not unlike the fields they had planted and cultivated back home on their Madison County farm.

According to the book, *Across the River: The People, Places, and*

Culture of East Athens, by Maxine Pinson Easom and Patsy Hawkins Arnold, at the time of the Seagraves' arrival, East Athens was considered "out in the country." As late as 1914, the *Athens City Directory* lists farmers living on Peter Street.

One of those farmers would be Hardy's son, Edward Pope "Fid" Seagraves, and one of the farmhouses listed in that city directory would be the Seagraves' Athens homeplace at 265 Peter Street.

Edward Pope "Fid" Seagraves and his nephew, Nelson "Petie" Seagraves, sitting on a cotton wagon at the Peter Street homeplace.

The family would have crossed the Oconee River covered bridge, built in 1856, to the more populated areas of Athens, where merchants sold goods, prosperous citizens built houses, and the University of Georgia, the oldest land grant university in the country, educated students from wealthy families.

Roads on both sides of the river were hard to navigate back in those days since they were not yet paved, and there was no electricity in the area. Having come from a rural farming community in Madison County, it is not hard to imagine Hardy and Andy hunting rabbits and other game in areas of East Athens that are now densely populated to provide for the Seagraves family.

Some structures standing in Athens when the Seagraves arrived include The Ware-Lyndon House, The Bank of Athens, and The Lucy Cobb Institute. Oconee Hill Cemetery, where Hardy, Andy, and many other Seagraves family members would, in years to come, be buried, opened in 1856.

Electricity wouldn't come to Athens until 1896, when Brumby's Drugstore downtown was lit up on December 12 using power generated by the new hydroelectric station at Mitchell's Bridge. We do not know if Hardy, Andy, and other Seagraves family members witnessed this momentous event, but if they did, it must have been a specular sight to see.[7]

Making A Living and Raising a Family in Athens

Hardy and Pink Carithers Seagraves on the grounds of their Peter Street house. In the background, to the right, is the chicken house.—From Freddy Seagraves

Like many residents of Athens in the mid-1800s, Hardy, Andy, and other family members were drawn to Athens by jobs in the textile mills. The Civil War devastated farms. Without income from crops, farm families needed jobs to survive. Hardy began working at an Athens textile mill as a teenager. He married Patience Pinkney Emma Carithers, who became known in the family as "Grandma Pink," on January 3, 1875.

Segraves/Seagraves

Family Tree

John Segraves & Martha "Patsy" (maiden name unknown) Segraves

|

William Issac Buchner "Buck" Segraves & Cheney Strickland Segraves

|

Noah Seagraves & Rebecca Williams Seagraves

|

Hardy Calloway Seagraves & Patience Pinkney "Pink" Seagraves

|

Charles Emory "Hard Charlie" Seagraves, Bessie Seagraves, Frederick "Fred" "Shack" Seagraves, Harvey Lee "Bob" Seagraves, Edward Pope "Fid" Seagraves, Lula Armenia Seagraves Hansford, Clela Mack Seagraves, Leonard "Len" Seagraves

In an 1880 U.S. Federal Census record, Hardy, twenty-nine, and Pink, twenty-one, are listed as living on Balderas (Baldwin) Street with Pink's widowed mother, Lucinda Carithers, forty-nine, Pink's younger sister, Parilie, fifteen, and Hardy and Pink's first three children, Bessie, five, Charles, three, and Fred, four months.

Pinkney Carithers "Grandma Pink" Seagraves in her later years

In a 1900 Census record, Hardy, forty-eight, is listed as owning the 265 Peter Street house that multiple generations of Seagraves remember fondly. Also living there were Pink, forty-one; Frederick, twenty; Edward "Fid," eighteen; Lula, fifteen; Harvey L "Bob," thirteen; Clela, five; and Leonard (misspelled as

Lindred), eleven months. The oldest son, Charles, had already left home, and the oldest daughter, Bessie, had already passed away as family legend says she died young. Hardy is listed as a night watchman.

Grandma Pink Carithers Seagraves' Family History

Clan Carruthers crest with the motto: Promptus et Fidelis (Ready and faithful)—From Clan Carruthers Profile. Scotclans.com. Retrieved 11 November 2014.

Patience Pinkney Emma "Pink" Carithers Seagraves is descended from Clan Carruthers, a Lowland Scottish clan. Their motto is "Promptus et Fidelis (Ready and faithful).

Clan Carruthers' tartan is a rich shade of red with deep hunter green and white accents. (The Carruthers' name also is spelled Carithers, and there are many other variations.)

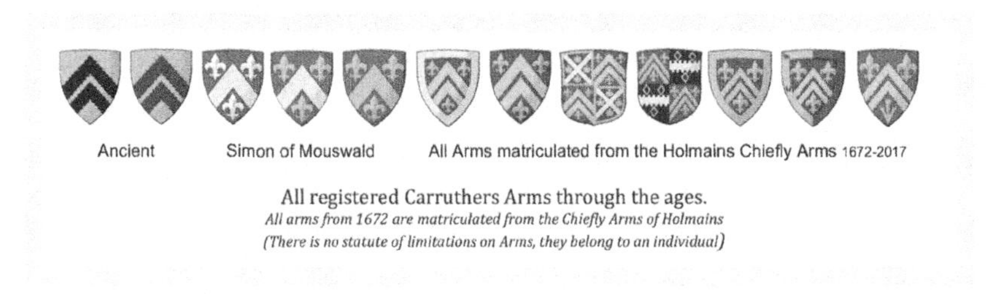

All the registered Carruthers Arms through the ages—From Wikipedia

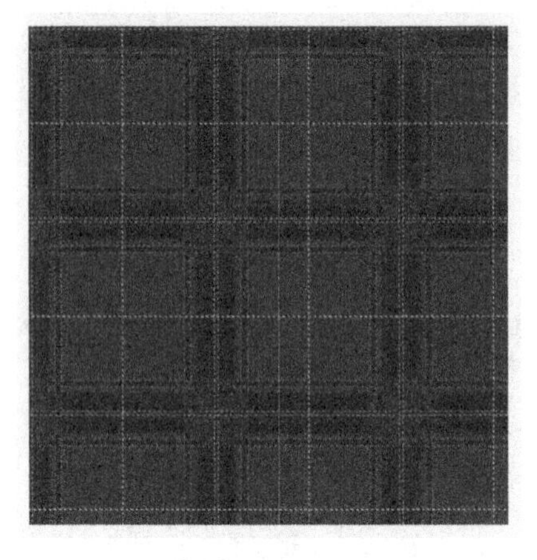

Carruthers Tartan—From Wikipedia

Pink Carithers Seagraves' Ancestors

Henry White
Born Apr. 24, 1724
Died June 17, 1802
in Bedford Co. Va.

married

Celia Page
Born Sept. 18, 1731
Died Mar. 31, 1799

They had twelve children
our direct ancestor was

Henry Page White
Born Sept. 21, 1756
Died July 30, 1842
a copy of his will is
attached to this paper

married

Martha Neville Brown
Do not have these dates
She was the daughter of
James Brown who came from
Scotland in 1740

They had three children

1 Elizabeth

2 Isaiah
Isaiah's wife was named
Mary (Polly) they lived
and died in Franklin Co.
Virginia. They had two
children

3 Lucy

Henry Page White

Martha Neville White
Married Willis H. Bennett
Nov. 21st 1829 in Va.
Franklin Co. They had ten
children

1. Lucinda V.A.F. 2. Akillis H.M. 3.Columbus W. 4. Martha (Patsy) 5.Mary
married
James Allen Carithers
A copy of this marriage record
is among these papers
6. Sarah J. 7. Madison Woods 8. Christopher W. 9. Amanda Paralee 10Ella

I believe that from this page and the others you can get your family record

Some Seagraves descended from Hardy and Grandma Pink have a significant amount of Scottish DNA, some of which is apparently from the Carithers family.

Lucy Bennett Carithers
Daughter of
Willis Bennett and Martha White Bennett

Lucy Bennett Carither's maiden name was Lucinda Virginia America France Bennett, her father was Willis H. Bennett and her mother was Martha Neville White (Bennett). Lucinda V.A.F. was called Lucy, was born March 1st, 1831 (and was born in Franklin County, Virginia) Her mother's father was Isaiah White and wife' name was Mary "Polly") Lucy Bennett married James Allen Carithers January 22, 1852 and they had seven children. Lucy died October 29th, 1913, James Allen her husband died during the Civil War At Dalton Georgia At the home of his sister who lived in Dalton at that time.

The children are as follows:

1. Elizabeth Carithers (died when very young, was the oldest child)

2. James (Jim) Carithers married Jane Smith
   Their children: Clarence, Dorsey, Mark, Jim, Candler, Ab

3. Martha A. Carithers married Joe a. Saye Sept. 26, 1878 by JC Johnson
   Their children: Ida Saye Herring, Norma Saye Smith, Susie, Ruby, Joe a. Jr. (M.) Ethel Richard, Maisie, Herbert, Earnest

4. Pink (born Sept. 1858, died June 27, 1931 married Hardy C Seagraves January 2, 1875, he died July 1, 1918 they had eight children
   Children: Bessie born Nov. 2, 1875 died July 9, 1895
   Charlie E. born Nov. 19, 1878 died Oct 4, 1934
   Fred born Feb. 12, 1880 died Mar. 21, 1950
   Ed. P. born May 15, 1882 died June 23, 1951
   Lula born Aug. 10,1884 died March 22, 1946 (Died June 30 PK.)
   Harvey Lee born Apr. 3,1888 died March 14, 1956
   Clela Mack born June 26, 1894
   Leonard Wood born June 18, 1899 died aug. 16, 1950

5. Sarah Frances married W.J.T. Baker February 10, 1878. She was born September 22, 1861 and died Feb. 24, 1931. They had six children.
   Their children: Ethel lee born March 15, 1879 m. J.T. Davis
   James Wiley born Aug. 1st 1881 m. died May 21st, 1936
   Grover Lamar born Jan. 18, 1885 m Bell Hayes
   Ernest Edward born Nov. 21, 1893
   Helene Bone born June 27, 1896

W.J.T. Baker died Sept. 7, 1919 at his home at Athens, Georgia where his family lived. This information was obtained from family Bible owned by Ernest Edward Baker, printed by Bradley & Co. 1876. It is in Ernest Eduard Bakers possession.

6. William Carithers married Mary Frances Carithers
Their children; Mattie Demonia m C. E. Landers
Cora Arbella m Lord
George Washington Carithers
Noble Hope Carithers

7, Paralee Carithers married James W. Giles, she was born
died Dec. 11, 1948. James W, Giles died October 18, 1939.
James W, Giles and Paralee E, Carithers were married January
10th, 1904 by Rev. W.M. Saye M. G. Recoredd in Book K page 303.
Coutrhouse at athens, Ga.

Georgia, Clarke County.

I certify that the above information is true as told to me by my mother and Aunt Paralee Giles and found in the Baker family recorded taken from the family Bible as given above

We are not sure who compiled these family history pages found in Anne "Annie D" Seagraves' papers, but from the comments on one of these pages, it was apparently one of Grandma Pink's nieces.

The Seagraves House on Peter Street

A 2022 photo of the former Seagraves family homeplace at 265 Peter Street—Photo by Donny Bailey Seagraves

The house at 265 Peter Street was a rambling farmhouse with a wide, wraparound front porch. Bessie Seagraves Kemp, daughter of Hardy and Pink Seagraves' oldest son, former Athens Police Chief Charles

"Hard Charlie" Seagraves, remembers sleeping on the porch in warm weather to stay cool in those long-ago days before homes were air-conditioned.

Here's a collection of items that came from the Peter Street homeplace. The glasses to the left may have belonged to Grandma Pink.—Photo by Phillip Seagraves

"It was so hot in the summer we slept out on my grandparents' porch on pallets (beds made from quilts and blankets). The speckled guineas hollered, and mosquitoes from the spring bit us all night long," Bessie Seagraves Kemp said in a 1980s interview with Donny Bailey Seagraves.

In Hardy's day, there was no indoor bathroom or running water at the Peter Street house. Family members used the outhouse and chamber pots and pumped water for cooking. A side door on the porch led directly into the large kitchen, which was the heart of the home with its farm table, stove, and icebox. This room almost always smelled like fried chicken, biscuits, and other Southern food favorites cooked by Grandma Pink and Aunt Clela.

A letter to Mrs. Pink Seagraves, East Peter St., Athens, Georgia, postmarked 1929

Clela Mack Seagraves

Clela Mack Seagraves—From Freddy Seagraves

Hardy and Pink's daughter Clela never married, though family legend says she may have been engaged at least once. She lived in the Peter Street house her entire life. Clela and her mother cooked endless cast-iron pots of peas, beans, and other vegetables grown in their garden. There was plenty of sausage and country ham, too, and biscuits and cornbread were daily staples at the Seagraves' house.

Clela Mack Seagraves—From Freddy Seagraves

Harold Frederick "Freddy" Seagraves, youngest son of Hardy and Pink's grandson Harold, spent a lot of time at Aunt Clela's house on Peter Street when he was young.

"I remember going out to the chicken house and catching a chicken for Aunt Clela to cook for supper," Freddy said. "She chopped off the head and threw the chicken out in the yard to flop around until it was dead.

Clela Seagraves holding her great-nephew Robert Edward "Bobby" Seagraves, older brother of Freddy Seagraves. In the background, to the left, is her brother Fid's pickup truck. Fid is sitting in the truck's passenger seat. The man talking to him is unidentified.—From Freddy Seagraves

"There was no indoor plumbing in that house back then, and I remember using the outhouse. I also remember sleeping in Aunt Clela's featherbed when I was very young and eating breakfast with Carl, Uncle Charles "Hard Charlie" Seagraves's son who lived at the Peter Street house.

"My dad, Harold Seagraves, brought Aunt Clela home to our house when she was sick, before she passed away. Later, we lived in Papa Bob's (Harvey Lee Seagraves) house on Grove Street, and I remember playing in his barn and pastures with neighborhood kids. We lived there for a few years after my daddy, Harold Seagraves, passed away."

Edward Pope "Fid" Seagraves

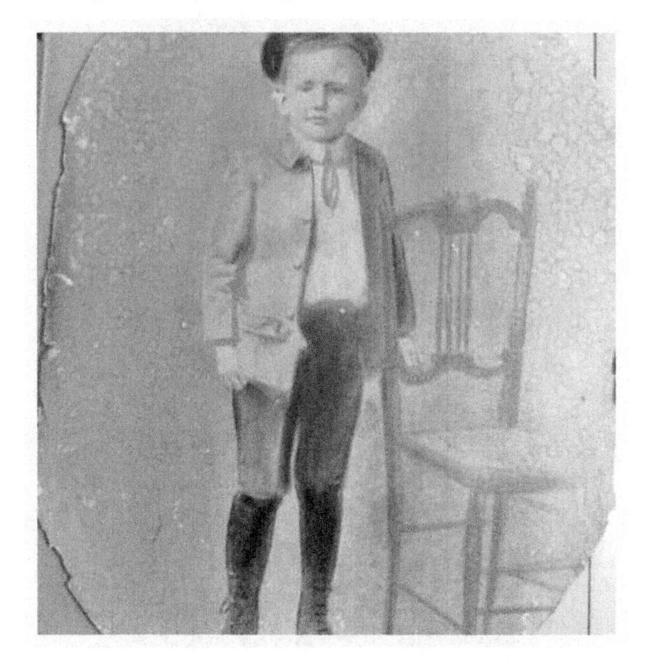

Here's a childhood portrait of Edward Pope "Fid" Seagraves that was found in the attic of an East Athens house.

Like his younger sister Clela, Edward Pope "Fid" Seagraves never married. However, he got a marriage license in 1927 to marry Laura C. Hammond, who is buried in Oconee Hill Cemetery, still bearing her maiden name.

He also never left home, though he owned many acres in Clarke County and became one of the area's most successful farmers and business owners.

Family members surmised that Fid's many years of declining health might have caused him and his sister Clela, who took care of Fid, to remain single.

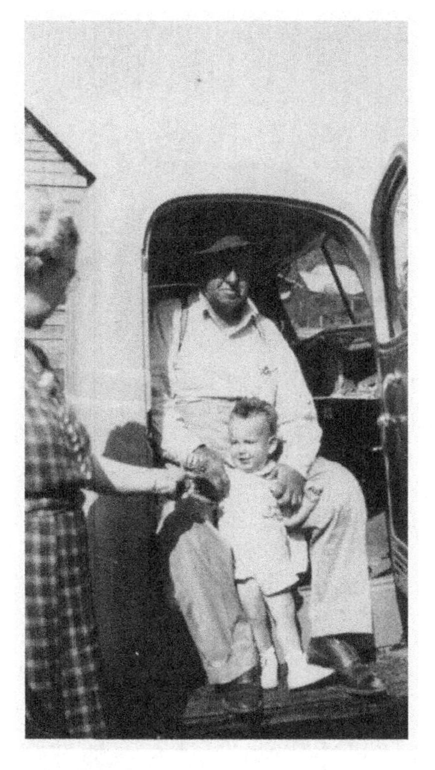

Edward Pope "Fid" Seagraves sitting in his beloved pickup truck with his great nephew Bobby Seagraves. Looking on is Clela Seagraves, Fid's sister.—From Freddy Seagraves

Fid had difficulty walking in his later years and conducted most of his farming business while sitting in the passenger side of his pickup truck. Since he could not drive, he paid others to do his driving for him. After Fid died in 1951, his family had an image of his beloved pickup truck engraved on his tombstone.

The Seagraves' homeplace on Peter Street stayed in the family for many years after Hardy and Grandma Pink died. At some point, Paul Bendzunas, a well-known glass artist, and his wife Barbara bought the house and operated their glass-blowing business there. They sold the home and property on June 29, 1990, to Michael Littleton, who was listed on Athens-Clarke County tax records as the owner at the time this book was written.

Edward Pope "Fid" Seagraves' gravestone at Oconee Hill Cemetery. Family legend says he loved his pickup truck so much family members had it engraved on his tombstone.—Photo by Donny Bailey Seagraves

Hardy Calloway Seagraves Dies

Hardy Calloway Seagraves and Patience Pinkney "Pink" Carithers Seagraves in what we believe is a composite portrait, two photographs put together after Hardy died.—Photo by Phillip Seagraves

Hardy Seagraves died on July 1, and his twin brother Andy died on July 16 during the Spanish flu pandemic of 1918. The following quote is from an article about Hardy Seagraves' death that appeared in the *Athens Weekly Banner* on July 5, 1918.

"Mr. (Hardy) Seagraves was a good citizen — quiet and unassuming, but holding firmly his convictions and always doing his duty as he saw it in any circumstances. He raised a large family of sons and daughters who honor his life and will cherish his memory — a strong tribute to the life of any man."

8

A sampling of Seagraves family graves at Oconee Hill Cemetery in Athens, Georgia. Bottom, L-R: Graves of Nelson "Petie" and Anne "Annie D Seagraves; grave of Andrew Mathew "Andy" Seagraves; Harvey Hill "Sleepy" Seagraves' grave. Top photos, L-R: Bridge in Oconee Hill Cemetery; Hardy and Pink Seagraves' graves; Oconee Hill Cemetery entrance across from Sanford Stadium.

Chapter 5

Salads

Suzanne Seagraves Gerling's Memories

I remember the moment I walked through the door of the little house on Georgia Drive, I felt at home. It was warm and always full of family. When I was really young, there was a furnace in the hallway that I would sit by with my sister Sandy; we sat by the warmth like it was our own personal fireplace.

Suzanne Seagraves Gerling visiting her grandparents at the house on Georgia Drive

Uncle Phillip, who still lived at home back then, would dress up in an old black top hat he'd gotten at a sale at the Bernstein estate and Grandpapa Pettyjohn's coat, and he'd be my special playmate. I can't recall the character's name he was impersonating, but we always had so much fun.

I got my first bicycle while we were visiting the family in Athens. Phillip rebuilt it and made it the envy of the neighborhood. With its white banana seat and unicorn purple/lavender color, it was the prettiest bike I'd ever seen.

The other thing I thought was great when we visited was sleeping on the cot in the living room. Dad would be on the sofa and he and I would watch horror movies on TV. Frankenstein was my favorite!

Christmas was magical in that small home on the hill, with the tree decked out with tinsel and those wonderful big colorful lights. They had treats and candy dishes on the table and there was always laughter.

Suzanne Seagraves Gerling with her grandmother Annie D on a long ago Christmas visit at the house on Georgia Drive

I can't remember any present in particular that I received there at Christmas, but we always left Athens and headed back home to Marietta, knowing that we had been with those who loved us. —*Suzanne Seagraves Gerling*

Suzanne Seagraves Gerling, daughter of Billy and Jo Seagraves, granddaughter of Nelson "Petie" and Annie D Seagraves and great-granddaughter of Harvey Lee "Bob" and Julia Suddeth Seagraves, was an award-winning equestrian during her younger days.

~

Fruit Salad and Dressing

- *2 cups fresh orange sections (bite size)*
- *2 cups diced pineapple (drained well)*
- *2 cups fruit cocktail (drained well, save juice)*
- *1/2 pound marshmallows (cut up)*
- *1/2 pint whipping cream*

Combine all ingredients for dressing (see recipe after these instructions), stirring constantly until thickened. Remove from heat and cool. Combine fruit and marshmallows in large bowl. Whip the cream and fold in the cooled salad dressing. Pour over fruit and blend. (Make a day ahead.)

Dressing for the Salad

- *2 eggs (beaten)*
- *2 tablespoons sugar*
- *Pinch of salt*
- *2 tablespoons lemon juice*
- *1/4 cup fruit juice*
- *1 tablespoon butter*

Combine all together and cook.—*Anne Seagraves, Clarke County, Georgia*

Martha Jo Dobbins Seagraves in her Marietta, Georgia kitchen with her mother-in-law Anne "Annie D" Seagraves

Reception Salad

- *1 box lemon Jello*
- *2/3 cup (chopped) celery*

- *2/3 cup (chopped) nuts*
- *1/2 pint whipping cream*
- *1 #1 can crushed pineapple*
- *1 8-ounce cream cheese*
- *1/2 teaspoon salt*

Drain juice from pineapple. Heat and dissolve Jello into hot juice. Let thicken and add other ingredients. Have cream cheese softened and cream whipped before adding to Jello mixture.—*Agnes Pettyjohn Russell, Whitfield County, Georgia*

Annie D with her older sister Agnes Pettyjohn Russell

Pasta Salad

- *1 pound cooked pasta (use your favorite - rinse with cold water)*
- *3 tablespoons olive oil*
- *3 tablespoons lemon juice*
- *2 teaspoons seasoning salt*
- *1 small can chopped black olives*

- *1 red and green bell pepper*
- *6 large green olives with pits*
- *3 tablespoons mayonaise*
- *Onion (optional)*

Mix all together and chill.—*Suzanne Seagraves Gerling, Coweta County, Georgia*

Nelson "Petie" Seagraves with his oldest son Billy Seagraves on the porch of the Seagraves house at 215 Georgia Drive. Petie used to say he got his nickname from playing with peewee marbles when he was a kid. We're not sure how he got the nickname "Petie" from peewee, but that's what he always said.—From Sandy Seagraves

Five Bean Salad

- *1 can wax beans*
- *1 can red kidney beans*
- *1 can green beans*
- *1 can lima beans*
- *1/2 cup chopped green bell pepper*

- *2 stalks chopped celery*
- *1/2 cup chopped Vidalia onion*
- *1 small jar pimentos, chopped*
- *1/2 cup salad oil*
- *2 cups sugar*
- *1/2 cup apple cider vinegar*
- *1 tablespoon salt*
- *1 teaspoon white pepper*

Open all cans of beans and drain in a colander. Mix (beat) well salad oil, sugar, vinegar and pepper. Place beans in a sealable container, pour mixture over beans, seal the container and marinate overnight in the refrigerator. Drain out some of the liquid. Bean salad is even better on the second and third days.—*Ann Seagraves, Madison County, Georgia*

Broccoli Salad

- *2 cups fresh broccoli*
- *1 small red onion, chopped fine*
- *1 cup raisins*
- *1 cup sunflower seeds or cashews*
- *3 strips bacon, cooked crisp and crumbled*
- *1 cup mayonnaise*
- *1/2 cup sugar*
- *1 tablespoon vinegar*

Toss all ingredients together. Mix mayonnaise, sugar, and vinegar and pour over broccoli.—*Ann Seagraves, Madison, Georgia*

Selected Seagraves school pictures from Oconee Street School. Bottom row, L-R: Mary Seagraves Fields; Frank Ed Seagraves; Rebecca Seagraves Baugh. Top row, L-R: Freddy Seagraves; Harold Seagraves and Phillip Seagraves.

Chapter 6

Soups

The Other Ann Seagraves

For several years, I wrote a weekly newspaper column that appeared on the editorial pages of the *Athens Daily News* long before the days of email and text messaging.

Seagraves Mill road sign in Madison County, Georgia—Photo by Phillip Seagraves

One day, I got a call from an Ann Seagraves. This Ann with the same name as my mother-in-law, who is the Annie D of this book, was from Madison County, Georgia, where our branch of the Seagraves family first settled during the early 1820s.

"I enjoy reading your columns," Ann said. "Tell me something. Are you related to me?"

A young Ann Shellnut Seagraves—From Tristin Seagraves Johnson

I had heard husband Phillip's Seagraves were related to the Madison County Seagraves who owned and operated Seagraves Mill. His dad, Nelson "Petie" Seagraves, used to talk about family barbecues his dad had attended, hosted in Madison County by Ford Seagraves, who once owned the mill.

The last Seagraves Mill building, on Seagraves Mill Road, off the Nowhere Road in Madison County, Georgia, was rebuilt in 1954, after the previous mill building washed away in a torrential rain.—From Tristin Seagraves Johnson

After I told Ann of Madison County the names of Phillip's family, she said she was sure they were related but didn't know exactly how.

Later on, Phillip was looking for a new location for our business, Seagraves Antiques, and wondered if we might rent the Seagraves Mill building. He had heard it was empty and possibly available.

Seagraves family members gathered in front of a historic Seagraves barn in Madison County, Georgia. L-R: May be Millard Seagraves, Weyman Seagraves, unidentified, unidentified, may be Kathryn Seagraves.—From Tristin Seagraves Johnson

"It's an out-of-the-way location and doesn't seem like a good choice for an antique shop," I said after he told me about his idea.

"Many antique collectors enjoy going on a hunt in out-of-the-way places," Phillip pointed out. "It's a fairly long ride to George Howington's shop in Bogart, but we enjoy going there. Bobby Bales' place, not too far from Seagraves Mill in the Sanford Community, is another off-the-beaten-path antique shop we like to visit, and so is Mozelle Lewis' Bargain Barn in Monroe."

Phillip called Ann, and she invited us to come take a look at the mill building. We drove to the Sanford Community and toured the dusty old structure a few days later. Although we could imagine our business there, we both agreed that maybe the location was a bit too remote.

Ford Seagraves' former house in Madison County, Georgia, one of the prettiest in the area, was built in 1850. Josiah Milsey Seagraves, Ford's father, purchased the house from John Pittman.—From Tristin Seagraves Johnson

Ann's house was down the road from the mill building, across from Seagraves Lake. Phillip knocked on her front door. She opened it and said, "Well, what do you think?"

"It's beautiful out here in the Madison County countryside, and we like the Seagraves connection," Phillip told her. "But it's a little too remote for us. We're going to pass for now."

"I understand your decision. Let's sit and visit for a while," Ann said, motioning us inside her house.

We sat in Ann's living room that day with a gorgeous picture window view of Seagraves Lake, the site of the original dam and mill building, and a popular Madison County fishing spot.

After comparing our Seagraves, we found that her husband, Arthur Weyman Seagraves' grandfather, Josiah Milsey Seagraves and Phillip's great-grandfather, Hardy Calloway Seagraves, were brothers. So Phillip's dad Nelson Hardy "Petie" Seagraves and Ann's husband Weyman Seagraves were first cousins, once removed.

During our visit, Ann gave me a copy of "The History of

Seagraves' Mill," an article written on January 15, 1954, by an unknown author.

"You might want to write about Seagraves Mill someday," she said.

Thanks to Ann all those years ago, you'll find "The History of Seagraves Mill" in chapter eight of this book.—*Donny Bailey Seagraves*

Anne's Own Homemade Soup

- *1 pound boneless beef (chuck or steer meat) cut into 1-inch cubes and salted with 1 teaspoon salt mixed with 1/2 teaspoon sugar*
- *2 cans tomatoes (mashed) and 2 cans water*
- *2 cans Veg-all and 2 cans water*
- *1 can green butter beans and 1 can water*
- *1 can green beans and 1 can water*
- *1 can small white peas and 1 can water*
- *1 pound okra (cut up)*
- *4 carrots (cut up)*
- *4 Irish potatoes (cut up)*
- *2 bay leaves*
- *1/2 bell pepper*
- *2 sticks celery (cut up)*
- *3 onions (chopped)*
- *2 cloves garlic (cut up)*
- *1 pod hot pepper - dark crushed red pepper*
- *Black pepper to taste*

Put all ingredients into a large boiler (pot) and cook for two hours, stirring occasionally. It makes a large potful, enough to freeze some for later.—*Anne Seagraves, Clarke County, Georgia*

Seagraves family members gathered for a meal in Annie's D's Georgia Drive kitchen. Front row, L-R: Suzanne Seagraves Gerling, Jo Seagraves. Back row, L-R: Sandy Seagraves, Joe Gerling.

Another Vegetable Soup

- *1 can of petite diced tomatoes*
- *1 bag frozen butter peas*
- *1 bag frozen okra, cut up*
- *2 carrots, cut into soup-sized pieces*
- *2 potatoes, cut into soup-sized pieces*
- *1 can crowder peas*
- *1 can yellow or white corn*
- *1 can pinto beans*
- *Any other vegetables you want*

- *Salt to taste*
- *Black pepper to taste*
- *Crushed red pepper to taste*
- *1 teaspoon sugar (optional)*
- *1 or 2 bay leaves*
- *1/2 to 1 teaspoon minced garlic*
- *2 or 3 tablespoons olive oil*

In front on the bicycle: Carol Pettyjohn Hitt with her cousin Mary Seagraves Fields. On the Georgia Drive house porch, L-R: Mabel Farr Pettyjohn, Luke Pettyjohn and Billy Seagraves.

Put all ingredients in pot and bring to a boil. Then simmer for about an hour, until potatoes are soft and the broth is rich.—*Donny Bailey Seagraves, Clarke County, Georgia*

Chicken Soup

- *1 whole chicken or 4 - 6 chicken breasts or several chicken thighs if you prefer dark meat. Note: You get a richer, better-tasting broth from a whole chicken.*
- *6 carrots, peeled and cut lengthwise in half and then on a diagonal*
- *4 stalks celery, cut on a diagonal*
- *1 large onion, cut up*
- *Salt to taste (I use about 1/2 - 1 tablespoon of sea salt.)*
- *Pepper to taste (I use about 1/4 to 1/2 teaspoon black pepper.)*
- *A sprinkle of crushed red pepper*
- *About a teaspoon of sugar (I use cane sugar.)*
- *1/4 to 1/2 teaspoon thyme*
- *1 or 2 bay leaves, depending on size*
- *1 cup of uncooked rice — not instant. (White tastes best. Brown is healthier. Sometimes I use both.)*

Boil whole chicken (or chicken pieces) in a large pot until done. (I usually use a whole chicken and boil forty-five minutes on one side, then turn the chicken and boil thirty - forty-five minutes longer.) If you use a whole chicken, remove any loose inner parts if they're inside the chicken.

When the chicken is done, let it cool. (You can put it in a metal bowl and put in refrigerator to speed up the cooling.) Then pull off meat and add it, broken into bite-sized pieces, to the pot. Add the vegetables, spices and the rice. Also, add more water to the pot if needed to bring the liquid level up near the top of the pot. Bring to a boil, then simmer about an hour, until vegetables are tender and broth is rich.—*Donny Bailey Seagraves, Clarke County, Georgia*

Chapter 7

Bread

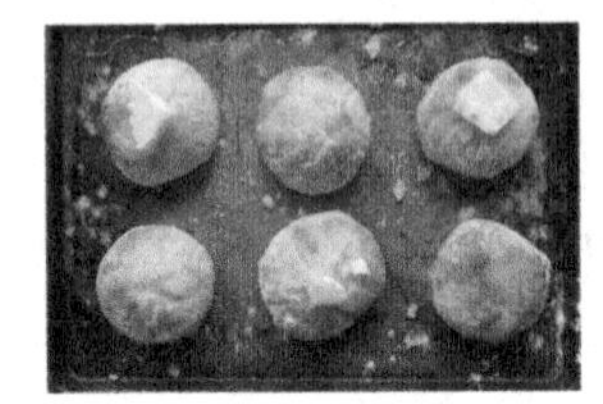

How Mom (Annie D) Made Biscuits

She first washed her hands and cleaned under her fingernails. Then she put flour in her wooden bread bowl, then added a scoop of lard (you could use a shortening such as Crisco).

Slowly, she poured in buttermilk and worked it gently through the flour and lard. She didn't do this too long, so the biscuits wouldn't be tough. She knew just how long to knead.

Next, she rolled the dough into small balls with her hands and patted them down on her old blackened biscuit pan.

Lastly, she patted the biscuits down more with her knuckles.

My mom's biscuits were her art form, and she cooked all things with love. She prided herself on cooking delicious and nutritious food for our family. There's nothing like her food today.—*Mary Seagraves Fields, daughter of Anne "Annie D" Pettyjohn Seagraves and Nelson Hardy "Petie" Seagraves*

We don't know what temperature Annie D used to bake her biscuits. Try preheating the oven to 425 degrees. Then bake for about 10-12 minutes or until the biscuits are golden brown.

Annie D and daughter Mary Seagraves Fields in the Georgia Drive house kitchen

Banana Bread

- *1 cup sugar*
- *1/3 cup cooking oil*

- *2 (beaten) eggs*
- *2 cups sifted plain flour (add salt and soda below to flour)*
- *1 teaspoon soda*
- *1/2 teaspoon salt*
- *1 cup (chopped) nuts*
- *3 or 4 ripe bananas (mashed)*

Mix sugar, eggs and cooking oil. Add bananas. Put flour in and add nuts. Pour into greased loaf pan. Bake at 350 degrees for one hour. *—Anne Seagraves, Clarke County, Georgia*

Anne "Annie D" Pettyjohn Seagraves

Banana Bread - Another Version

- *1/2 cup butter*
- *1 cup sugar (I use cane sugar.)*
- *2 eggs, beaten*
- *4 bananas, coarsely mashed with a fork*
- *1 1/2 cups flour (I sometimes use white and occasionally whole wheat or a combination of those two types of flour.)*

- *1 teaspoon baking soda*
- *1/2 teaspoon salt (omit the baking soda and salt if you use self-rising flour)*

Preheat oven to 350 degrees. Cream together with a fork butter and sugar. Add beaten eggs and mashed bananas. Combine well. (I use a big spoon rather than an electric mixer.) If using plain flour, sift together flour, soda and salt. Add to creamed mixture. Mix until just combined. Do not over-mix.

Pour into a greased loaf pan. Bake at 350 degrees in oven for fifty-five minutes or until desired doneness. I stick a knife into the middle after fifty-five minutes, and the banana bread is done if it comes out clean. If not, I cook it five or ten more minutes.

You can add walnuts or pecans if wanted.

Let banana bread cool, then wrap in tinfoil and store in the refrigerator. Can be frozen.—*Donny Bailey Seagraves, Clarke County, Georgia*

PawPaw's Sweet Biscuit

- *A biscuit*
- *Syrup (your favorite or whatever you have on hand)*
- *A finger*

The simplest Seagraves recipe I know came from Pawpaw, Weyman Seagraves. If you remember, Weyman was missing a forefinger. I can't remember if it was his left or right, but one was just a stub. I thought it was the neatest thing.

Well, Pawpaw's recipe for a sweet biscuit was to poke a hole in one and pour syrup into it. Turns out, he did that one too many times. He claimed that's how he lost his finger. He said he wore it off, poking holes in biscuits to pour syrup in.

Pawpaw's finger was really chopped off with an axe, I believe.

Donny Bailey Seagraves

My husband says my dry humor comes from the Seagraves in me. —*Tristin Seagraves Johnson, Sullivan County, Tennessee, originally from Madison County, Georgia*

Ann and Weyman "Pawpaw" Seagraves, "cutting up" in their Madison County, Georgia kitchen—From Tristin Seagraves Johnson

Cornbread

- *1/2 stick of Crisco (or 1/2 cup of Crisco from the can)*

Put the Crisco into a COLD iron skillet and put this skillet in a COLD oven. Then turn on the oven and set it to 450 degrees. Watch the heating skillet in the oven carefully and quickly remove it and put on top of the stove as soon as the shortening is all melted and before it starts smoking or catches fire.

A young Weyman "PawPaw" Seagraves on a horse in Madison County, Georgia—From Tristin Seagraves Johnson

While the shortening is heating, combine in a medium metal bowl:

- *2 cups of cornmeal mix*
- *2 cups of buttermilk*
- *2 eggs*

Make sure it's a metal bowl, not glass. Stir this and combine well.

After you take the hot cast-iron skillet with the melted shortening out of the stove, carefully pour about half of the melted shortening into the other ingredients in the metal bowl. Stir it all together until well-blended.

Holding the hot handle of the iron skillet with a potholder and move the skillet in a back and forth circular motion, swirling the remaining melted shortening around inside the skillet until the insides of the skillet are coated. Then pour the ingredients into the metal bowl. Bake the cornbread in the skillet in the oven at 450 degrees for twenty-five minutes. (More or less time, depending on how your oven cooks.)

Let cornbread cool in the skillet for a few minutes, then remove. To remove from skillet, I loosen cornbread underneath with a heat-safe spatula. Next, I put a large plate on top of the cornbread and turn the skillet over so cornbread is on plate. If some sticks, slide spatula underneath and fit it on the top of the cornbread in the crust-missing places. Sometimes we put cheese or butter inside the warm cornbread. This cornbread goes well with chicken soup or chili. —*Donny Bailey Seagraves, Clarke County, Georgia*

How Agnes Simmons Coile Made Cornbread

> "The following cornbread recipe is from Agnes Simmons Coile and is shared here by her daughter Judith Coile Donohoe. Agnes was my maternal grandmother and Judith is my aunt. Grandmother Agnes's husband, Albert Odell Coile, was a son of Mahulda "Hulda" Strickland Coile, a sister of Reba Seagraves' mother. This cornbread recipe may have come down to my grandmother from the Simmons family, the Coile family, or the Strickland family, or perhaps she created it from a combination of those family recipes. It is similar to Annie D's cornbread recipe."
>
> — Donny Bailey Seagraves

Preheat oven to 450 degrees. My mother used an iron skillet, but they're too heavy for me, so I use a nonstick baking pan or muffin tin.

Add oil to pan (to coat), and heat it in the oven for five or so minutes, so the batter will sizzle when poured in.

Use white cornmeal only, self-rising (I do prefer the buttermilk kind). Add buttermilk (whole or 1%), about 1/4 cup of oil blended into batter, mix well. Eggs are not needed. (*Note: No amount was specified for the cornmeal - try a couple of cups and adjust if needed.*)

Albert Odell Coile with his mother Mahulda Jane "Hulda" Strickland Coile (1880 - 1958). Hulda was a sister of Evalena Goss Strickland Wynn (1879 - 1958), mother of Harvey Lee "Bob" Seagraves' second wife, Susie Reba Winn Seagraves.—From Coile family photo albums

My mother always added some of the heated oil to the batter. I can't tell that it makes a difference. Pour batter with or without some of the heated oil into pan or tin and bake for about 20 minutes at 450 degrees (depends on your oven temperature, of course). Turn down the heat to 375 degrees and bake for about ten or fifteen more minutes.

Insert a knife into the center, if needed, to check for doneness in the middle. You'll also know by the fragrance that it's done. Turn out onto a plate, butter, and consume.

Sorry I don't measure, but neither did my mom Mary Agnes Simmons Coile.—*Judith Coile Donohoe, Wake County, North Carolina, originally from Clarke County, Georgia*

Annie D's Cheese Cornbread

- 3 cups cornbread mix
- 1 1/2 cups milk

- 3 eggs
- 1 onion, grated
- 1 cup grated sharp cheese
- 2 tablespoons oil
- 1 can whole corn (drained or vacuum packed)
- Small carton sour cream

Grease a nine by thirteen by two-inch pan. Mix all ingredients except for sour cream, reserving some grated cheese. Pour mixture into pan, then spoon dollops of sour cream on top. Sprinkle with remaining grated cheese. Bake at 350 degrees for thirty minutes.—*Anne Seagraves, Clarke County, Georgia*

Seagraves family members gathered in the Georgia Drive house kitchen for a long ago holiday meal. Clockwise, L-R: Annie D, Petie, Billy, Donny, Jo.

Chapter 8

Seagraves Mill

The following "History of Seagraves Mill," once located off Nowhere Road on Seagraves Mill Road, was given to me by Ann Shellnut Seagraves over thirty years ago. Ann's husband, Weyman Seagraves, was the last Seagraves family owner of Seagraves Mill. The author of this mill's history is unknown. Many thanks to Ann Seagraves for sharing this article with me so I can now share it with you.—Donny Bailey Seagraves

The History of Seagraves Mill

Prior to the year 1800, a settler by the name of Vandifer came to Georgia, settling at what was then known as Little Sandy Creek, Madison County, Georgia. The site at which he built was near an old Indian free-flowing rock-basin spring, which had once served as assembly grounds for Indian tribes.

Vandifer built a log cabin near this spring, and he later realized the need for a mill in the vicinity to grind grain for settlers. He then built a dam over the creek and a small log mill house where he installed a paddle-type water wheel. The early settlers came to the mill with their corn to be ground, some traveling to and from the mill on horseback.

Strickland Builds A New Mill House

In 1840, Vandifer sold his farm and mill to Richard Strickland. Mr. Strickland operated the mill for a short time, later selling it to his son, Washington Strickland. Since the mill was built, the surrounding community had increased in population considerably, and Mr. Strickland realized the need to increase the capacity of the mill in order to also grind wheat for flour. In 1860, Mr. Strickland began construction of a new mill house, which was the same mill house in operation at the time this history was written.

An old gristmill similar to Seagraves Mill—Photo by dssimages

They built the new mill house around the old log structure, which was torn down piece by piece and carried out by hand. At this same time, they installed a stone flour mill; the stone used being a

French Burr Stone, which had been imported from France about mid-century.

Ancient stone wheel from a gristmill—Photo by Milijan Zivkovic

In the operation of the flour mill, the wheat was bolted (sifted) through a hexagon reel twenty feet long. Three grades of flour were made: heads (from the top part of the wheat plant where the kernels are), middlings (the product of the wheat milling process that is not flour), and shorts (the fine bran particles, germ, and a small portion of floury endosperm particles separated in the usual processes of commercial flour milling).

They constructed the second mill house of forest heart timber, the sill (the bottom horizontal member of a wall or building to which vertical members are attached) being twelve by twelve and forty feet long and of one solid log. The first and second plates (a horizontal, structural, load-bearing member in wooden building framing) were, likewise, only smaller in dimension. The floor was made of one-and-one-half-inch hand-dressed heart timber, not being nailed but pegged to the sleepers (short walls used to support floor joists, beams, and block or hollow slabs at ground floor). This same flooring is still in use (at the time this history was written), although it is now, of course, showing wear in places from foot tracks, etc.

A Seagraves family barn, near Seagraves Mill in the Madison County, Georgia Sanford Community—From Tristin Seagraves Johnson

The first timber used in the building was cut on the farm by a sash saw operated by a water wheel at the waterfalls above the mill, where the dam stood in 1954. At the time of the mill house building, oxen teams hauled the logs from the forest to the mill. The weather-boarding and the floors of the mill house were hand-dressed by a smoothing hand plane, and wooden pegs pinned the framework. The weatherboarding put on at that time (1860) is the same weather-boarding on the building in 1954. However, the roof has been renewed from time to time.

R. L. Pittman Buys the Mill

In 1882, R. L. Pittman purchased the mill property from the estate of Washington Strickland. Mr. Pittman was a great sportsman, owning many bloodhounds, bird dogs, and racehorses. He employed mostly prisoner labor under the lease system of convicts. Mr. Pittman also was a crack shot with a gun and usually carried two 45-colt revolvers in a holster on his belt.

During Mr. Pittman's ownership of the mill, he built a dirt dam across the creek, making a reservoir of approximately 10 acres of water, which was used as a surplus water supply for grinding.

An old gristmill gear—Photo by MizC

Also, during Mr. Pittman's ownership, a Star Mail Route was established in 1890, running from Danielsville, Georgia, to Nicholson, Georgia, stopping at the mill twice per week. The mill-house was selected as the Post Office and was given the name of Monitor, Georgia. Farmers from two or three miles around came to the mill to get their mail from this point. The pigeonholes where the mail was placed were still in the mill in 1954.

Josiah Milsey Seagraves Buys the Mill

Mr. Pittman continued operation of the mill until 1906, at which time the mill property was purchased by J. M. (Josiah Milsey) Seagraves. Operation of the mill was continued, using the same wheat and corn rock. In 1914, A. F. (Arthur Ford) Seagraves purchased the mill. He was still the owner in 1954 when this history was written.

This Seagraves Mill painting was painted by Mary George Poss, an Athens, Georgia artist who once studied under Lamar Dodd and Howard Thomas at the University of Georgia.—From Tristin Seagraves Johnson

In 1922, the old dam was raised four feet, increasing the water power supply. A steel overshot wheel was installed, furnishing power for the mill until 1946. In 1940, a modern roller mill fifty-barrel had been installed. Then, in 1946, the steel overshot wheel was replaced by two modern turbine wheels to furnish power for the mill.

The dam was raised again, this time eight feet, making a water reservoir of approximately forty acres. This, of course, gave the mill a greater supply of water. The dirt and wood race was also replaced by steel pin stocks, extending through the dam and into the mill house, preventing water loss by leakage.

Weyman and Ann Shellnut Seagraves and their three sons, Todd, John and Mark—From Tristin Seagraves Johnson

This McCormick Deering Thresher was found in the woods behind Ann Seagraves' Madison County house and may have been used as one of the first steps in the process of getting different grades of flour.—From Tristin Seagraves Johnson

The most remarkable feature about this mill is that in its 150 years of operation, it had (in 1954) never once been shut down, except for repairs, which have consumed only a very brief period of time. Thousands of bushels of corn have been processed at this mill site during the years of its operation, furnishing old-fashioned water-ground meal to the community.

The same principle of grinding used 100 years ago is still in use, except for the wheat grinding, which was transferred to a more modern processing method. Old-fashioned water ground meal and whole wheat flour, plain and self-rising, are processed at the mill, and custom grinding is done by hammer mill for the farmers in this vicinity. The quality of the cornmeal is so popular that people moving out of the immediate vicinity of the mill into other communities, even to other states, often order their meal and have it sent to their new location.

Seagraves Mill Liquor Still

An old still—Photo by Ben Whitaker

During the many years of the mill's operation, it became a community gathering place where farmers, bringing their corn and wheat to the mill on Saturdays, would stop to chat over the events of the week. Many stories have been handed down concerning occurrences at the mill, one of the most amusing being about the liquor still in the branch at the rear of the mill. As the story goes, the proprietor of this still would make a run of whiskey and then take the still out of the branch and put it into a corner of the mill until the next operation.

Seagraves Mills Water Ground Corn Meal truck—From Tristin Seagraves Johnson

At the present time (1954), an enrichment system is being installed, on runner rocks (huge stones used to grind grain into flour, cornmeal, grits, or feed for livestock), in order to give the cornmeal and flour the proper enrichment (which adds nutrients that were removed during milling). At the beginning of the operation of this mill, grinding was done for only a few customers in the community, and gradually that increased, year by year, until, at the present time, more grist, wheat, corn, and feed is processed than in any past years.

Ann and Weyman Seagraves of Madison County, Georgia. Weyman, a son of Ford Seagraves and grandson of Josiah Milsey Seagraves, was the last Seagraves to own and operate Seagraves Mill.—Photo from Tristin Seagraves Johnson

The mill property also has become a landmark of the Sanford Community, Madison County, and, besides being a historic spot, is also one of scenic beauty, the public and community having access to a wayside park and spring, which is widely visited, not only by the community but by people from various parts of the country who travel great distances.

Seagraves Lake in Madison County, Georgia—From Tristin Seagraves Johnson

The reservoir of approximately forty acres, used mainly for a surplus water supply, is also stocked with most all game fish such as bass, brim, and catfish. The lake is a beauty spot of the community, being located in lovely wooded surroundings and many people avail themselves of the opportunity to fish and picnic.

Mr. Ford Seagraves, the present owner (in 1954), welcomes visitors to inspect the old mill, use the wayside park, rest under the shade of trees and enjoy the beauty of nature.[1]

The last Seagraves Mill building. This picture was taken in 2021.—From Tristin Seagraves Johnson

Historic Seagraves Corn Meal Returns

For many years, grocery stores in Madison County and surrounding areas carried a popular local product, Seagraves Corn Meal, produced at the historic Seagraves Mill in Madison County, Georgia.

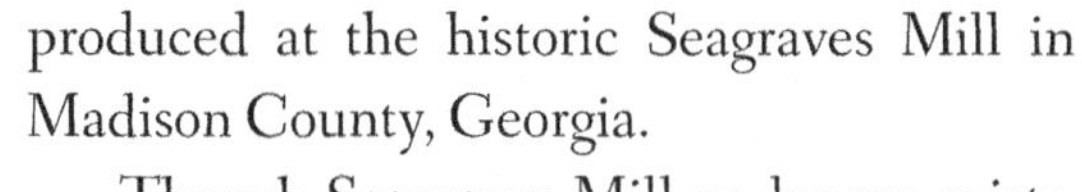

Seagraves Corn Meal—Photo from Todd Burroughs

Though Seagraves Mill no longer exists, Seagraves Corn Meal is once again available and is now produced and sold by B&G Seed Company.

Visit http://www.bgseed.com to read more about Seagraves Corn Meal, including an article written by Wayne Ford for the Athens Banner-Herald, published November 21, 2015.

Seagraves Mill Lake

A big catch at Seagraves Lake in Madison County, Georgia—From Tristin Seagraves Johnson

Another Madison County landmark is Seagraves Mill Lake, a historic and notable body of water in the Sanford Community of Madison County, Georgia, about 4.5 miles from Nicholson, on Seagraves Mill Road. Madison County owns the dam, but the Seagraves family privately owns the lake and its shores.

Although it was an essential part of Madison County's history, while this book was being written, Seagraves Lake was drained because of unfunded repairs required under new guidelines in the Georgia Safe Dams Act.

Many Madison County residents and others have pleasant memories of Seagraves Lake. Perhaps future Seagraves will find a way to refill the lake so that they and others can once again enjoy fishing and picnicking there.[2]

Ann Shellnut Seagraves, age 90, with her great-granddaughter Madi and granddaughter Tristin Seagraves Johnson. Tristin is a great-great-granddaughter of Josiah Milsey Seagraves, a great-granddaughter of Arthur Ford Seagraves, granddaughter of Weyman Seagraves and daughter of Todd Seagraves.—From Tristin Seagraves Johnson

Chapter 9

Main Dishes

Jen Seagraves' Memories

I remember my grandmother Anne's kitchen in several incarnations. My earlier memories as a child between five and twelve involve chicken mull and sausage biscuits.

Also, she made a special candy during the holidays called divinity. It was a very sweet candy that was pure sugar, yet it was light, fluffy, and as thin as air. My grandmother whipped it into little bite-sized chunks that looked like white, fluffy clouds. Sometimes she added chopped nuts, but I preferred it without nuts.

Something special about how divinity was made "the right way" is that it had to be done on a day when it was not too humid or when it wasn't raining, or it wouldn't "set up." It would flop and flatten out if grandmother Anne made it on the wrong kind of day. Divinity was a rare treat that we enjoyed, and it was always special when she made it on the right day for the right occasion, such as Thanksgiving or Christmas.

Other memories of grandmother Anne's kitchen are from when I was a teenager, fourteen to eighteen, and she would make a big

Seagraves' family members enjoying a meal together in Anne's Georgia Drive house kitchen. Front row, L-R: Donny Bailey Seagraves, Greg Seagraves, Jen Seagraves. Back row, L-R: Jo Seagraves, Mary Seagraves Fields, Phillip Seagraves. Standing at the stove is Travis Fields.

"Sunday dinner" (lunch) after church. The meal usually consisted of Southern staples such as fried chicken, ham, and vegetables like green beans, squash casserole, mashed potatoes and gravy. There was always a dessert such as cake or pie — pound cake was my favorite.

Another favorite food that grandmother Anne cooked for me was cornbread dressing at Thanksgiving. She had a way of making it I haven't been able to emulate. It was always the right consistency — not too dry and not too wet. I also loved her biscuits and want to try making them like she did.

One more thing I remember was my grandmother's sweet tea. She made it with saccharine, and it always had a very distinctive taste and an elevated level of sweetness. Having come up during the time of the Great Depression, she reused old milk jugs for her tea. She would scald them out, sanitize them, put her tea mixture in the jugs, and shake them up.

I loved the house on Georgia Drive. As a child, I remember there would always be food, desserts, or candy available when we visited. Grandma Anne had an old icebox in the kitchen where she used to keep pantry items, including snacks.

Anne "Annie D" and Nelson "Petie" Seagraves' granddaughters in the Georgia Drive house kitchen with cakes on the table and to the right, divinity. L-R: Jen Seagraves, Sandy Seagraves, Lori Fields Loden (seated at the table) and Suzanne Seagraves Gerling.

Jennifer "Jen" Seagraves and her grandmother Anne "Annie D" Seagraves in a composite photo that shows their family resemblance. Jen is the daughter of Phillip and Donny Bailey Seagraves, granddaughter of Nelson "Petie" and Anne Pettyjohn Seagraves and great-granddaughter of Harvey Lee "Bob" and Julia Suddeth Seagraves. She is a dual-degree graduate of the University of Georgia.—Photo from Jen Seagraves

Her kitchen was very 1940s and the vintage of the house. It was warm and inviting, with a round oak table in the middle where we would sit, eat, and enjoy the wonderful food she prepared for us. Cooking and eating was and still is a time to gather and connect over a meal made with pride and love. I believe my grandmother Anne genuinely loved to cook and make food for her friends and loved ones.—*Jen Seagraves*

~

Chicken Casserole

- *1 (10-ounce) package frozen chopped broccoli, thawed*
- *3/4 cup cooked rice*
- *2 cups cooked diced chicken*
- *2 cups cream of chicken soup (2 cans)*

- *1 1/2 teaspoon lemon juice*
- *1/2 cup mayonnaise*
- *1/2 cup grated cheddar cheese*

Mix all together real good. Put in a casserole dish. Bake at 350 degrees for thirty-five to forty-five minutes.—*Anne Seagraves, Clarke County, Georgia*

> "On Christmas mornings when I was a kid, my grandfather Papa Bob (Harvey Lee Seagraves) would come by for an early morning visit at our Georgia Drive house to see what Santa brought. Then we gathered around the kitchen table for a fried quail with biscuits and gravy breakfast. In his younger days, my dad Petie hunted quail. Later on, he bought quail for our traditional holiday breakfast. I always looked forward to that special meal. This family tradition may have been passed down from my great-grandparents Hardy and Pink Seagraves." [1]
>
> — Phillip Seagraves

Another Chicken Casserole Recipe

- *8 - 9 chicken breasts*
- *2 cans cream of chicken soup*
- *8 ounces sour cream*
- *1 stick margarine*
- *1 stack from box Ritz Crackers*

Cook chicken and cut into small pieces. Spray Pam on a nine-by-thirteen-inch baking dish. In a large mixing bowl, combine chicken pieces, cream of chicken soup, and sour cream. Spread evenly into baking dish. Crumble Ritz Crackers over casserole. Melt one stick of margarine and pour evenly over the casserole. Preheat oven to 325 degrees and then bake for thirty to forty minutes.—*Ann Seagraves, Madison County, Georgia*

How Agnes Simmons Coile Made Chicken and Dressing

Start by baking an iron skillet or pan of cornbread (see my mother's cornbread recipe in chapter seven or use another cornbread recipe of your choice). Then, after it's done, cut some out and remove — enough to make room for broth, chopped onions, and celery. Cut remaining cornbread into chunks.

Into the chunked cornbread, mix chicken broth (approximately three boxes or make your own stock), one chopped onion, and chopped celery to taste.

Add sage and thyme to taste. (This recipe makes a whole pan, so don't skimp on veggies or herbs.) The consistency should be somewhat liquid but not floating in broth — it will dry out during baking, of course, but you want it to still be moist when it's baked, not dry.

Agnes Simmons Coile visiting with Annie D in the mid-1980s—Photo by Donny Bailey Seagraves

Sprinkle a little paprika on top if you want — it looks good and adds a tiny bit of heat. Bake for 30 - 45 minutes at 425-450 degrees (turn down to 350 the last few minutes, if need be) until it smells like my mother's dressing (or someone else's dressing you remember from childhood) and it's a bit browned around the edges.

Before baking, you can also add pieces of cooked chicken or a whole chicken into the dressing, then bake. Some dressing may have to be removed before you bake if you add a whole bird (as my mother usually did). The removed dressing can be added to the cornbread you took out earlier and a second pan of dressing made.

Note: It may or may not take the entire three boxes of broth. Depends on how much cornbread you make!—*Judith Coile Donohoe, Wake County, North Carolina — originally from Clarke County, Georgia.*

Travis Fields, son of Mary Seagraves Fields and Jimmy Fields and grandson of Anne "Annie D" Seagraves and Nelson Hardy "Petie" Seagraves, and great-grandson of Harvey Lee and Julia Suddeth Seagraves, loves chicken mull and is an expert at cooking it. He learned everything he knows about chicken mull from Annie D.

Chicken Mull

- *4-pound fryer or 4 pounds of chicken parts*

Have a large pot to put chicken in. Use water to cover chicken real good, almost to the top of pot. Boil chicken until it is real tender. Add to the chicken these ingredients while cooking:

- *3 or 4 large onions*
- *2 cloves garlic*
- *2 bay leaves*
- *Pinch of oregano*
- *1/4 teaspoon crushed red pepper*

When done, remove chicken from broth and let it cool, then chop into bite-sized pieces. Be sure no bones are left in the broth. Put two quarts sweet milk in broth. Also, one stick of margarine. Add chicken to milk and margarine and let come to real slow boil. Boil about twelve minutes. Put on simmer. Add about three packs of broken soda crackers. Season with one teaspoon salt, one tablespoon black pepper, one or two tablespoons of vinegar and one-half cup of catsup. Serve hot with crackers, onions, sliced tomatoes, and pickles, sweet or dill.—*Anne Seagraves, Clarke County, Georgia*

"Chicken mull is a traditional dish from North Carolina, upstate South Carolina and Georgia. Though we don't know for sure, perhaps Hardy Seagraves' ancestors brought their chicken mull recipe from North Carolina to Madison County, Georgia, where our branch of the Seagraves first settled. In the 1950s and 1960s, chicken mull often was served at political rallies, fundraisers and community celebrations. The Seagraves family often cooked and served chicken mull. Some family members still do."[2]

— Donny Bailey Seagraves

Chicken Mull – Another Version

- *2 or 3 large fryers (save broth)*

Boil until real tender. Add four or five large onions, two garlic cloves, two bay leaves and pinch of crushed red pepper. Add to chicken while boiling. Remove from broth when done. Cool. Take all bones out. Chop chicken into chunks or pieces. Put broth in the boiler. Add two quarts of sweet milk and one-half to one stick of margarine. Let milk and margarine come to a slow boil and boil about twelve minutes.

Put on simmer. Add chicken and cook at a slow boil for a few minutes, then add crushed soda crackers, three packs or more, according to desired thickness. Season as you desire with salt, black pepper, catsup, and one-fourth cup to one to two tablespoons of vinegar. Serve hot with crackers, bread, onions, sliced tomatoes or pickles (your choice).—*Anne Seagraves, Clarke County, Georgia*

~

Seagraves Descendant Mark Ed Hansford

Mark Ed Hansford, former owner of the Chase Street Cafe in Athens, Georgia

Mark Ed Hansford, son of Allan and Sarah Hansford, grandson of Mark C. and Lula Seagraves Hansford, and great-grandson of Hardy and Pink Seagraves, was a well-known Athenian. He owned and operated the Chase Street Cafe, an Athens institution that his parents passed down to him.

The modest building wasn't much to look at, but inside the place was clean and filled with tantalizing aromas of Southern-style country cooking, very similar to what you would have smelled at the Seagraves homeplace on Peter Street in East Athens back in the day.

"Whatcha gonna have?" Mark Ed would yell from his place behind the counter as customers arrived. Usually, he would have your plate ready right after you sat down. Speedy service was one of his specialties.

Stew and Q, a popular lunch special at Chase Street Cafe

One of the most popular specials at the Chase Street Cafe was "stew 'n cue, which included a bowl of chicken mull and a barbecue sandwich, both Seagraves family favorites from way back. There are two chicken mull recipes in this book. We don't know the Mark Ed Hansford chicken mull recipe, but most likely it was one of the two in this book, a combination or something very similar. On the other hand, his chicken mull recipe could have come from his Hansford family. Either way, Mark Ed's chicken mull, barbecue, and other Southern favorites he served at the Chase Street Cafe kept his customers coming back.

Mark Ed Hansford passed away on February 11, 2015 and that was also the end of the Chase Street Cafe. His obituary in the *Athens Banner-Herald* said: "He served in the United States Marine Corps, was the owner of Chase Street Cafe for over 28 years, and was a member of East Athens Baptist Church. Mark was a dad, an uncle, a brother, a grandfather, a marine, and police officer, but most knew him for his unique style of connecting with people at Chase Street Cafe.

"Though it has since closed and was a small family restaurant, it was not obscure and made a huge impact in the community. Mark fed everyone from trash collectors to the President, all sitting side by side. And he didn't distinguish between the two or treat one differently than the other.

"Whether you were blue collar or white collar, White or Black, young or old, rich or poor, you knew he was your friend. And you knew he would joke with you or even poke at you, all with the best intentions."[3]

~

L-R: Nelson "Petie" Seagraves and his grandson Kevin Fields and granddaughter Lori Fields Loden

Quick Chicken & Dumplings

- *3 chicken breasts*
- *2 or 3 flour tortillas*
- *1 can cream of chicken soup*
- *1 can chicken broth*
- *Salt and pepper*

Boil chicken, cool. Refrigerate the broth overnight. Drain fat from broth and bring to a boil. Add the soup and the one can of broth and chopped chicken. Cut the flour tortillas into one-by-two-inch pieces. Drop the tortilla pieces into boiling broth, occasionally stirring for about ten minutes. Let sit a few hours before eating to allow the tortillas to absorb the broth.—*Ann Seagraves, Madison County,*

Georgia

Phillip Seagraves in a Georgia Natural Gas Company publicity photo for a long ago Old Stove Round Up ad campaign

Chicken and Dumpling Casserole

Preheat oven to 350 degrees

Note: Do not stir (layer into nine by thirteen-inch baking pan)

- *4 chicken breasts - cook and chop or use rotisserie chicken*
- *2 cups chicken broth*

- *1/2 stick butter*
- *2 cups Bisquick*
- *2 cups whole milk*
- *1 can cream of chicken soup*
- *3 teaspoons chicken granules*
- *1/2 teaspoon dried sage*
- *1 teaspoon black pepper*
- *1/2 teaspoon salt*

Melt butter and pour over chicken, then sprinkle with black pepper and sage - do not stir. Mix milk and Bisquick and pour over chicken layers. Mix two cups chicken broth and chicken soup and pour over Bisquick. Bake thirty to forty minutes at 350 degrees until golden brown.—*Ann Seagraves, Madison County, Georgia*

Hardy Calloway Seagraves was named after two of his ancestors: Hardy Segraves and Calloway "Callie" Segraves. Other names frequently passed down in the Segraves/Seagraves family include William, John, Nelson, Josiah and Milsey/Milzey. Josiah Milsey Seagraves, first Seagraves owner of Seagraves Mill, received two favorite family names. In Nelson "Petie" Seagraves' part of the family, his youngest son, grandson and great-grandson all have "Nelson" as their middle name.

Chicken Pie

- *4 - 5 chicken breasts*
- *1 can cream of chicken soup*
- *1 can cream of celery soup*
- *1 stick margarine*

- *1 cup milk*
- *1 cup self-rising flour*
- *Salt and pepper*

Annie D in her Georgia Drive kitchen. Yes, her dress does match her curtains!

Cook chicken breasts until tender and reserve one and one-half cups chicken broth. Spray nine-by-thirteen-inch baking dish with Pam. Cut chicken into bite-sized pieces and spread into baking dish. Preheat oven to 350 degrees. Melt one stick of margarine and allow to cool but not solidify.

In a boiler, combine one and one-half cups chicken broth plus one can of cream of celery soup, salt and pepper. Heat and stir until smooth, and then pour over chicken pieces in the nine-by-13-inch dish. Combine melted stick of margarine with one cup milk and self-rising flour and stir until smooth. Pour gently over chicken pieces and celery soup into the nine-by-thirteen-inch baking dish. PLEASE DO NOT STIR! Bake at 350 degrees for thirty minutes.—*Ann Seagraves, Madison County, Georgia*

Salmon Loaf

- *1 large can of salmon*
- *1/3 cup chopped celery*
- *1/2 cup fine bread crumbs*
- *1/2 teaspoon salt*
- *Pepper to taste*

Sandy Seagraves with her dad William Harvey "Billy" Seagraves in the Georgia Drive house living room

Flake salmon. Combine other ingredients and mix thoroughly. Put into small greased loaf pan. Sprinkle with paprika. Bake forty-five minutes in 350-degree oven.—*Anne Seagraves, Clarke County, Georgia*

Spaghetti Sauce

- *3/4 pound or 1 pound ground beef*
- *3/4 cup (chopped) onion*

- *1 (chopped) garlic clove*
- *1 2/3 cups tomato sauce (large can)*
- *1/2 teaspoon oregano leaves*
- *1/4 teaspoon black pepper*
- *1/2 teaspoon salt*

Brown beef with onions and garlic in large skillet. Drain off excess fat. Add other ingredients. Heat to boiling and then reduce heat and simmer fifteen minutes. Serve over cooked spaghetti.—*Anne Seagraves, Clarke County, Georgia*

Jen Seagraves and her mom Donny Bailey Seagraves, cooking in their Winterville kitchen.—Photo by Phillip Seagraves

Turkey and Black Bean Chili

- *1 pound ground turkey (best to use is 97/3)*
- *1 can black beans (no salt or low salt)*
- *1 can diced tomatoes (no salt or low salt)*
- *1 green bell pepper (diced)*
- *1 onion (chopped - yellow or Vidalia)*
- *1/2 to 1 tablespoon sea salt*
- *1/4 to 1/2 tablespoon black pepper*

- *1/2 to 1 tablespoon sugar (optional)*
- *bay leaf*

Put about one-half cup oil (your choice) in a three- or four-quart pot. Add onion and bell pepper and sauté until soft. Add ground turkey and cook until done (no pink left). Add the tomatoes and one-half can of water. Add the black beans and one-half can of water. Stir, then add the salt, pepper, sugar, bay leaf and bring to a boil. Reduce heat to low, cover the pot, and simmer for thirty minutes.

Top with shredded cheese, if desired. This chili tastes great with crackers or cornbread and a green salad. It's great leftover and freezes well.—*Donny Bailey Seagraves, Clarke County, Georgia*

Kevin Fields, oldest son of Mary Seagraves Fields and Jimmy Fields, enjoying a long ago meal in the Georgia Drive house kitchen. He is a grandson of Nelson "Petie" and Anne "Annie D" Seagraves and great-grandson of Harvey Lee "Bob" and Julia Suddeth Seagraves.—Photo by Donny Bailey Seagraves

Chicken Chili

- *3 chicken breasts*
- *1/2 chopped onion*
- *2 cans green chilis*
- *2 cans navy beans*
- *1/2 pint fat-free Half and Half*
- *1/2 teaspoon cumin*
- *1 tablespoon chili powder*
- *Salt and pepper*
- *One package shredded cheese*

Boil one whole chicken (or three chicken breasts). Reserve one cup of chicken broth. Cut chicken into small pieces. Into a cooking pot, place cooked and cut chicken pieces, one cup chicken broth, one-half cup chopped onion, two cans chopped green chilis, two cans navy beans or your choice of white beans, one pint fat-free Half and Half.

Mix and bring to a boil; reduce heat and simmer. Add one-half teaspoon cumin, one tablespoon chili powder, salt and pepper to taste. Sprinkle shredded cheese on top, if you desire.—*Ann Seagraves, Madison County, Georgia*

Bottom row photos, L-R: Suzanne Seagraves Gerling and her husband Joe Gerling; Nelson "Petie" Seagraves and his son Phillip Seagraves; Annie D Pettyjohn Seagraves with son Phillip Seagraves. Top row photos, L-R: Betty Brooks and Mary Seagraves Fields (on bicycle); Billy Seagraves; Travis Fields.

Chapter 10

Meats, Fish, Seafood

Anne Seagraves Catches a Large Shellcracker

I knew this report was coming, as I had heard of it previously so today, here it is. Showing one of the best catches in this vicinity that I've heard of this season is Mrs. Nelson (Anne) Seagraves. It's a dandy!

It's a shell cracker that weighed right at two and a half pounds. She and her husband were fishing a private lake in Oglethorpe County when Mrs. Seagraves made her catch. Anne says she decided to have it mounted. She fished right on the bottom and used pink worms for bait.

Anne Seagraves Catches
A Large Shellcracker

GREAT
OUTDOORS

Athens Banner Herald
newspaper clipping found in Annie D's papers

She and Nelson fish together quite a bit, but today's catch really put Nelson down at the foot of the class. He caught one catfish and no definite weight was given. It was estimated to weigh about half a pound.

Anne was all pepped up over her catch, as if Santa Claus had paid her a visit. Congratulations Anne on your very good catch. —*Source:* Great Outdoors column by T. ED Williams in an undated edition of the *Athens Banner-Herald*.

Anne "Annie D" Seagraves fishing at a local lake. As usual, her rod and reel is either on the ground or on a stand as she patiently waits for a bite.

"Every now and then, Anne would call and invite us to come over for a boiled shrimp supper with her and Pete. Athens, Georgia, is over 200 miles from the coast, so a shrimp supper meant Anne had been shopping at Wilfong Brothers Seafood, where the shrimp, fish and other seafood arrived fresh each week. When Phillip and I walked into the house on Georgia Drive, the smell of boiled shrimp greeted us. We'd sit at the kitchen table with Anne and Pete, feeling rather coastal as we peeled shrimp and chatted about what we'd all done that day."

— Donny Bailey Seagraves

Boiled Shrimp

- *2 pounds fresh or frozen shrimp*
- *5 cups water*
- *1/4 cup salt*
- *1/4 teaspoon crushed red pepper*
- *1 garlic clove*
- *1 small onion*
- *2 bay leaves*

Add salt, crushed pepper, garlic, bay leaves and onion to water. Bring to a boil, then add shrimp and reduce heat. Cover and simmer three to five minutes. Shrimp is cooked when center is done and when it turns pink and floats to the top. Drain shrimp and rinse thoroughly under cold water. — *Anne Seagraves, Clarke County, Georgia*

"Annie D didn't leave us any fish recipes, though she often went fishing and cooked her catch. Catfish and bream were our favorites. She cooked these fish the usual Southern way, breaded with a flour/cornmeal mixture and fried in hot oil or grease in a black iron skillet. Usually, Anne served the fish with a tossed salad, rather than coleslaw, along with hushpuppies. We all loved Anne's fried fish, and it was a real treat to be invited over for a fish dinner in her Georgia Drive kitchen."

— Donny Bailey Seagraves

Nelson "Petie" Seagraves, third from the left, with a bountiful catch from the Oconee River, circa 1940s. These are mostly catfish, but someone caught at least one shell cracker that day.

Harmon Jackson's Sausage

The top portion of a Jackson Grocery calendar found many years ago in the Seagraves' Peter Street homeplace—From Billy Seagraves

Annie D's Harmon Jackson's Sausage recipe came from Jackson's Grocery. This popular east-side Athens store opened in 1923 at 480 Oconee Street, within easy walking distance of the Seagraves' Georgia Drive home.

To each 100 pounds of meat, add:

- *20 ounces salt*
- *10 ounces sugar*
- *4 ounces black pepper*
- *2 1/2 ounces Dalmation sage*
- *2 1/2 ounces crushed red pepper*

This is for medium hot sausage. To get hot, use a little more pepper.

Mix pork at the rate of forty pounds of firm fat to sixty pounds of lean. Spread the meat out on a flat surface, sprinkle each seasoning over the cut meat and turn enough to get the meat and seasoning well mixed. It's now ready for the chopper.—*Shared by Anne Seagraves, Clarke County, Georgia*

> "Daddy used to say the day he and Mom got married, he only had about a dime in his pocket. They went down the hill to Harmon Jackson's store and bought a Coke and crackers and that's what they had for supper on their wedding night."
>
> — Mary Seagraves Fields

---

1 Hour Turkey or Hen

Rub butter all over the turkey or hen. Then rub salt, pepper and paprika all over it. Preheat oven to 500 degrees. Put turkey or hen in large roasting pan with top. If you don't have a lid, put foil over the pan and seal around the edges. Before doing this, add one cup water.

Do not open oven door for one whole hour. Cut oven off when hour is up and leave turkey inside. You can leave it in the oven all night if you plan to have it the next day.—Anne Seagraves, Clarke County, Georgia

London Broil or Flank Steak

- *1 clove garlic, minced*
- *1 tablespoon salad oil*
- *2 teaspoons parsley flakes (fresh or dried)*

- *1 teaspoon salt*
- *1 teaspoon lemon juice*
- *1 teaspoon pepper (I don't put a whole teaspoon)*

Poke the steak liberally! Pour the ingredients over and rub in. Broil or grill five minutes on each side.—*Anne Seagraves, Clarke County, Georgia*

~

Take the Girls Fishing

Mary Seagraves Fields and her brother Billy Seagraves fishing long ago, perhaps in the Oconee River.

According to a recent *Knight Ridder News Service* report, President George Bush takes his thirteen-year-old grandson but not, ahem, his seven- and eleven-year-old-granddaughters on fishing trips.

So now we know the truth: Our president, the highest-ranking official in the land, practices fishy discrimination when it comes to the females in his own family.

Does that sound fair, girls?

Bush tried to explain this difference in grandchild treatment by pointing out that his grandson "plays ball and does stuff" that his granddaughters apparently don't do.

Oh, come on, George. Have you asked the girls to go fishing with you?

At our house, fishing is a genderless activity. Everybody goes — but me. Though I am always invited, I usually decline the opportunity. Frankly, I see no value (other than a possible fish dinner) in so much boring, sweaty, waiting for uncertainty.

But I do value my invitation to indulge in this primitive form of entertainment and food gathering. If anyone excludes me from a family activity, I want that person to be me.

The more I think about it, the more I seriously doubt that a fish ever stops to ponder whether a girl or boy has just dropped a juicy bit of bait into the lake. The fish bites at it whenever the spirit (or is it merely hunger pangs?) moves him — or her. And, yes, it can be a him or a her when you reel in your catch. Fish families don't discriminate on the basis of sex. They allow all their children and grandchildren — males and females — to go fishing.

Jen Seagraves with a big catch!

My ten-year-old daughter Jenny is proud of her fishing skills, just as proud as her twin brother. She can cast and wait with the best of 'em, and she treasures her new Zebco 33 Rod and Reel just as much as her twin brother Greg treasures his.

Phillip Seagraves fishing with daughter Jen Seagraves at Thompson's Lake—Photo by Donny Bailey Seagraves

Jenny's favorite part of fishing is catching the fish. When I asked her why, she said, "It feels good to catch one." Then she added, "Last time we went fishing, I caught a catfish and a little bream, and Greg didn't catch anything."

"Ah, she's just bragging," Greg insisted. "Time before last, I caught six fish — and a log."

Of course, Greg imitates his dad when they fish together, and he feels a special closeness to him as they stand side by side in the buggy, ninety-nine-degree fresh air, two tough men casting their baited hooks into the crystal waters of Mrs. Nation's lake out in the wilds of Oglethorpe County.

Despite my disinterest in the sport, Jenny has a great female fishing role model to follow: her paternal grandmother Annie D Seagraves. Anne is a fisherwoman from way back, and she can hold her own with any man when it comes to reeling in the big ones. She even has a trophy — a huge, vicious-looking shell cracker — mounted and hung in a prominent spot over her kitchen door, well-deserved proof that girls can fish, too.

Greg Seagraves showing off a big catch!

Jen Seagraves fishing with her grandmother Annie D at one of her favorite area lakes. Anne loved to fish with her grandchildren and other family members.

Maybe it's time for President Bush to give his granddaughters a chance. Who knows, they might even catch all the fish. Perhaps that's the real reason Granddaddy Bush doesn't take those girls fishing.[1]

Seagraves' family members love to fish! Bottom row, L-R: Phillip Seagraves fishing with son Greg at Thompson's Lake; Greg Seagraves fishing with son George at Thompson's Lake; Greg Seagraves showing off a big fish. Top row, L-R: Melissa Seagraves fishing with son Patrick at Thompson's Lake; Nelson "Petie" Seagraves fishing; Phillip Seagraves showing off a big fish he caught.

Chapter 11

Barbecue

Seagraves Family Barbecues

From the early 1900s to the late 1940s, the East Athens Seagraves family was well-known for their annual barbecues on the grounds of the Seagraves homeplace on Peter Street. They raised hogs, chickens, and other livestock. When hog-killing time came, Edward Pope "Fid" and his brothers slaughtered hogs and processed meat in the front yard. Nearby, Fid Springs ran red with blood from the slaughtered animals.

They always reserved one hog (or more) for the family barbecue. Fid and his brother Leonard "Len" would roast the hog (or hogs) outside over an open fire. Other family members and friends would join in, helping to prepare endless side dishes, including fresh vegetables from the Seagraves' garden.

Cooking barbecue was an all-night affair that included the partaking of plenty of home-brewed spirits and lots of laughter and conversation. After meat was ground and other ingredients added, everyone took turns stirring hash with a long-handled wooden ladle in a giant black iron pot.

"I remember going to family barbecues at the Seagraves homeplace on Peter Street and watching my uncles cook all night long. The last time I visited that house, cousin Bobby Seagraves, Uncle Harold's oldest son, and I spent the night there in one of those big bedrooms. Aunt Clela cooked us a delicious meal that day – she was the best cook. Not long after, in 1959, Aunt Clela died."

— Billy Seagraves

Young Seagraves family members at a long ago Seagraves barbecue at the Seagraves homeplace on Peter Street. Bobby Seagraves is in the back row, first left. Next to him is Billy Seagraves. David Seagraves is on Billy's right and next to him is Judd Farr. Others unidentified.

The Seagraves version of hash was heavy on ground beef and pork and did not include corn, peas or potatoes. They made a vinegar-based barbecue sauce, which is typical of Georgia's sauces. The barbecue aromas drifting through the East Athens air during Seagraves barbecues must have been intoxicating back in the day.

"My favorite part of the Seagraves' barbecues was the special Seagraves barbecue sauce," remembers Bessie Seagraves Kemp, a daughter of former Athens Police Chief Charles Emory "Hard Charlie" Seagraves and a granddaughter of Hardy and Pink Carithers Seagraves.

A group photo from a Seagraves barbecue on the Peter Street house grounds, circa 1940s. On the third row, are the Seagraves' siblings, Lula Seagraves Hansford (third to the right), then Leonard "Len," Fred "Shack," Fid, Bob and Clela. Next to Clela is Rebecca Seagraves Baugh. Next to the end on that row is Gaynelle Seagraves Farr Wansley and husband Dick Wansley. Barbara Seagraves Tiller Carter is on the second row, first left. Frank Ed Seagraves is behind Fid to the right with wife Sarah next to him. Luke Pettyjohn is on the fifth row, fifth from the right with Nelson "Petie" Seagraves next to him. There are many other Seagraves and Hansfords plus friends and neighbors of the Seagraves in this photo.

"I've tried to make it many times over the years, but I've never gotten the proportions just right. They made it from salt, black pepper, red pepper, real butter, lemon juice and vinegar. My uncles Len and Fid Seagraves always made the sauce."

Bessie remembered Madison County cousins, including Seagraves Mill owner Ford Seagraves, a son of Josiah Milsey Seagraves, granddaddy Hardy's brother, coming to the barbecues.

Six Seagraves siblings, sons and daughters of Hardy and Pink Seagraves, at a long ago family barbecue: Front row, L-R: Edward Pope "Fid" Seagraves, Lula Seagraves Hansford, Fred "Shack" Seagraves. Back row, L-R: Harvey Lee "Bob" Seagraves, Clela Seagraves and Leonard "Len" Seagraves.

"My uncles Shack (Fred), Bob (Harvey), Fid (Edward) and Len (Leonard), and aunts Clela and Lula were always there. My daddy came to all the barbecues in the early days. He died in 1934."[1]

Seagraves Bar-B-Que Sauce

- *1/2 gallon vinegar (don't use white vinegar)*
- *1/2 pound pure butter*
- *1 heaping tablespoon crushed red pepper*
- *3 tablespoons black pepper*
- *3 tablespoons salt*
- *1 big lemon*

Harold and Mary Fred Warwick Seagraves' children and grandchildren attending a Farr - Seagraves family reunion on July 14, 1991. L-R: Lynn Seagraves holding her son Josh. Lynn passed away in 2006. Next is Lisa Seagraves Layne with her son Trevor, who passed away in 2019, and Bobby Seagraves, who passed away in 1998. Not pictured is Freddy Seagraves, Harold and Mary Fred's youngest son, who didn't attend the reunion that year. Bobby, Freddy, Lynn and Lisa are grandchildren of Harvey Lee "Bob" and Julia Suddeth Seagraves and great-grandchildren of Hardy and Pink Carithers Seagraves

Put all ingredients in large boiler and heat, stirring. Simmer for a while. Don't let sauce boil. Sample the sauce, then add more salt and black pepper to taste, if needed. Cut the big lemon and squeeze the juice into the sauce. Stir and simmer until it's the way you like it. —*Anne Seagraves, Clarke County, Georgia*

Donald Seagraves, David Seagraves and Billy Seagraves enjoying a long ago Farr—Seagraves family reunion.

Hash

- *12 pounds boneless (chuck) beef*
- *4 pounds pork (Boston butt)*
- *5 pounds onions*
- *12 (1 pound) cans tomatoes - pureed*
- *1 tablespoon crushed red pepper*
- *1/4 cup vinegar*
- *1 1/2 tablespoons black pepper*
- *1/2 pound butter*
- *1 tablespoon salt*
- *Black pepper*

Cook onions, red pepper, beef and pork altogether. Have enough water to cover meat good (lots). Cook this meat until it is real tender (save meat broth).

Puree tomatoes in blender and cook tomatoes separately for about one hour and fifteen minutes or until they look like mush. Keep stirring tomatoes to keep them from sticking.

Grind meat after it cools and put back in broth. Add cooked tomatoes, black pepper, salt, butter and vinegar to taste. Be sure to turn off heat while adding seasonings. Return to low heat to let it season.—*Anne Seagraves, Clarke County, Georgia*

L-R: Billy Seagraves, his father Nelson "Petie" Seagraves and Petie's nephew Judd Farr, Jr. at a long ago Farr - Seagraves family reunion in South Carolina. Judd is the son of Juddie Farr, Sr. and Gaynelle Seagraves Farr Wansley, grandson of Harvey Lee "Bob" and Julia Suddeth Seagraves and great-grandson of Hardy and Pink Carithers Seagraves.

Barbecued Leg of Lamb

- *5 to 10 pounds leg of lamb*
- *1/2 cup Worcestershire sauce*
- *1/4 cup orange juice*
- *1 tablespoon prepared horseradish*
- *Salt and pepper*
- *1/4 cup tart jelly*
- *2 teaspoons grated orange peel*

Sprinkle lamb with salt and pepper. Roast in pan at 325 degrees for twenty minutes per pound or until meat thermometer registers 140 degrees for rare, 160 degrees for medium or 170 degrees for well done. Meanwhile, in a saucepan, blend remaining ingredients. Simmer for five minutes. Brush lamb with sauce frequently during roasting.—*Anne Seagraves, Clarke County, Georgia*

Oven Bar-B-Que Chicken

Barbecue Sauce for the Chicken

- *1/4 cup vinegar*
- *3/4 cup ketchup*
- *1 teaspoon salt*
- *3 tablespoons black pepper*
- *3/4 stick butter*

Put ingredients in boiler and just let come to boil and then take off stove. Pour over chicken and cook at 325 degrees for one and one-half to two hours.—*Anne Seagraves, Clarke County, Georgia*

Judd Bernard Farr, Jr. and Farr - Seagraves Family Reunions

For many years, the Seagraves family held annual barbecues on the Peter Street homeplace property in East Athens. After Hardy and Pink Seagraves' children died, there were no more barbecues until Harvey Lee "Bob" Seagraves' grandson, Judd Farr, Jr., son of Bob and first wife Julia's daughter Gaynelle Seagraves Farr Wansley and J. B. Farr, Sr., began a new family tradition of

Judd Farr preparing barbecue Seagraves' style at a long ago Farr - Seagraves family reunion. David Seagraves is in the background.

hosting annual Farr - Seagraves family reunions at his South Carolina lake house, Farr Away Places.

Six Seagraves siblings and their first cousin at a long ago Seagraves - Farr family reunion at Farr Away Places in South Carolina. Front row, L-R: Nelson Hardy "Petie" Seagraves, his cousin Bessie Seagraves Kemp, daughter of Charles Emory "Hard Charlie" Seagraves, Gaynelle Seagraves Farr Wansley. Back row, L-R: David Seagraves, Barbara Seagraves Tiller Carter, Rebecca Seagraves Baugh, Donald Seagraves.

Judd "J.B." Farr, Jr. lettered in football, track and basketball at Athens High School and won scholarships in track and basketball at the University of Georgia. After college, he became one of the most devoted Bulldog fans and received the Dan Magill Award, which is given for "loyalty, dedication and commitment to the Bulldogs and the University of Georgia."

Judd was recognized with the "Old Faithful Dawg" Award and for 25 years served thousands of Bulldog Fans and cheerleaders at his famous tailgate. He also was a well-known businessperson who owned a beer distributorship for many years.

Judd and Betty Farr with their children and grandchildren in 1997

Besides his many accomplishments, Farr and Seagraves family members remember Judd as the family reunion host who cooked and served Seagraves family-style barbecue and all the trimmings and brought us together every year to reminisce.[2]

Chapter 12

Papa Bob and His Children

Harvey Lee "Bob" Seagraves

Harvey Lee "Bob" Seagraves, a son of Hardy and Pink Carithers Seagraves, distinguished himself as Superintendent of Climax Hosiery Mill, as a City of Athens First Ward Councilmember for twenty-five years, and as a City of Athens Mayor Pro-tem.

He was a native of Athens and a member of East Athens Baptist Church. He served as a deacon and, for many years, was known as one of the church's most active members.

As an Athens City Councilmember from the First Ward, Bob always worked energetically for the best interests of his ward and the city. During his many years on the council, he played a prominent role in the progress that came to Athens and the surrounding area.

Bob and his brothers owned a farm off U.S. Highway 78 East. Barbara Seagraves Tiller Carter remembered her uncle and aunt, Mark and Lula Seagraves Hansford, living on the Seagraves farm when she was young. Nelson "Petie" Seagraves used to talk about spending summers on the farm with his siblings and cousins, working in the fields, picking peas and other crops.

Harvey Lee "Bob" Seagraves received a gold watch after retiring as a City of Athens First Ward Councilmember.

The Seagraves donated a portion of their farm property for the construction of Gaines Elementary School. Later on, other land from the Seagraves farm became Cedar Creek subdivision.[1]

Tragedy in the Family

Bob experienced tragedy early on when his first wife, Julia Suddeth Seagraves, and her brother, Frank Suddeth, died the same night in 1918 from pneumonia brought on by the Spanish Flu, a horrible pandemic that followed World War I. During the flu pandemic, Bob also lost his father, Hardy, and his uncle Andy.

Frank Suddeth, Mary Akins Suddeth, Julia Suddeth Seagraves in an undated portrait. Julia was Harvey Lee "Bob" Seagraves' first wife.

Julia left behind five young children: Gaynelle, Harvey, Frank Ed, Nelson, and Harold. Julia and Frank's mother, Mary Akins

Suddeth, a widow who had been living with her son before his death, moved into the Seagraves home and took care of her four oldest grandchildren for several years after their mother died.

The youngest child of Bob and Julia Seagraves, Harold, was only about a year and a half old when his mother died. His aunt Clela, sister of his grieving dad Bob, took young Harold to live at the Peter Street homeplace where she and his uncle Fid raised him as if he were their son.

Bob and Julia met when they were young and attended school together at the Athens City School. Miss Ophelia Hilliard presented this school photo dated 1898 to their grandson Freddy Seagraves, youngest son of Harold and Mary Fred Seagraves, November 18, 1959. Mary Julia Suddeth is on the second row, second from the right. Harvey Lee "Bob" Seagraves is on the fourth row, third from the left.—From Freddy Seagraves

Julia and Frank are buried near each other in Oconee Hill Cemetery. Their mother, Mary Akins Suddeth, is also buried near her only children. We do not know what happened to Mary's husband, Andrew Frank Suddeth, his first wife, also named Julia, or where they are buried.

Harvey Lee "Bob" Seagraves Marries Again

A few years later, on March 20, 1922, Harvey Lee "Bob" Seagraves married Susie Reba Winn. During the next several years, they welcomed four more children to the Seagraves family: Rebecca, Barbara, Donald and David.

Harvey Lee "Bob" and Susie Reba Winn (originally spelled "Wynn") Seagraves about 1928—From Hope Seagraves Austin

Harvey Lee "Bob" Seagraves, known as "Papa Bob" to his children and grandchildren, died March 14, 1956. His widow, known as "Mama Reba" to her children and grandchildren, died March 13, 1986. They are buried in Oconee Hill Cemetery.

Harvey Lee "Bob" and Reba Winn Seagraves—From Hope Seagraves Austin

Harvey Lee "Bob" Seagraves' Children

Bob Seagraves raised a large family of three daughters and six sons with his first wife, Julia, and second wife, Reba.

Lillian Gaynelle Seagraves Farr Wansley

Gaynelle Seagraves Farr Wansley and husband Dick Wansley in Annie D's Georgia Drive house kitchen many years ago

Gaynelle Seagraves Farr Wansley was the oldest child and only daughter of Harvey Lee "Bob" Seagraves and his first wife, Julia Suddeth Seagraves. She lost her mother at age ten and her first husband, Juddie Bernard Farr, Sr. (see his profile in chapter 13), in a tragic firetruck accident when they were young. She and Juddie Farr, Sr. were the parents of Julia Farr DeRose Holzworth and Judd Bernard Farr, Jr. For most of her life,

Gaynelle was heavily involved in the Athens, Georgia community, and she was an early advocate for women's rights.

Gaynelle married again; her second husband was Dick Wansley. She died September 24, 2002, and is buried in Oconee Hill Cemetery. When this book was written, Gaynelle's Athens Five Points house was still in the family.

Harvey Hill "Sleepy" Seagraves

L-R: Nelson "Petie" Seagraves and his older brother Harvey Hill "Sleepy" Seagraves opening presents during a long ago Christmas party at the Seagraves house on Georgia Drive—From Sandy Seagraves

We do not know how Harvey Hill "Sleepy" Seagraves, oldest son of Harvey Lee "Bob" and Julia Suddeth Seagraves, got his "Sleepy" nickname, but we can guess that perhaps he enjoyed sleeping. Sleepy was born on December 20, 1909. When he was eight years old, his mother died. Sleepy attended the City School in East Athens and worked at Climax Hosiery Mill for many years. Later, he was employed at Chandler's Grocery Store on Oconee Street.

Sleepy collected guns and cruised around Athens in a 1962 white four-door Cadillac Sedan Deville. According to family legend, he had at least one serious romance when he was young, but Sleepy remained a lifelong bachelor.

Annie D often invited Sleepy to eat a home-cooked meal in her Georgia Drive house kitchen. Like the rest of us, he loved Anne's cooking. Sleepy died on March 3, 1984, and is buried near other family members in Oconee Hill Cemetery.

Frank Edward Seagraves

Frank Ed Seagraves as a young man, walking in downtown Athens, Georgia, near the Southern Mutual Building, which was later renamed The Fred Building.—From Missy Seagraves Jackson

Frank Ed Seagraves, a son of Bob and Julia Seagraves, was only six-years-old when his mother died. According to his sister Rebecca, he had a nickname, Gobby, when he was young. Gobby might have meant Frank Ed talked a lot.[2]

A veteran of WWII, Frank Ed worked many years for the City of Athens Police Department, rising through the ranks to become a captain. He married Sarah James, and they had a son, Frank Edward "Butch" Seagraves, Jr. Frank Ed died November 7, 1970, at age 58, and is buried in Evergreen Memorial Park.

Frank Ed Seagraves with wife Sarah James Seagraves and their son Frank Edward "Butch" Seagraves, Jr.

Nelson Hardy "Petie" Seagraves

Front row, L-R: Frank Ed Seagraves, Phillip Seagraves, Nelson "Petie" Seagraves. Back row, L-R: Billy Seagraves, David Seagraves, Donald Seagraves

Nelson "Petie" Seagraves, husband of Annie D and a son of Harvey Lee "Bob" and Julia Suddeth Seagraves, was born in Athens, Georgia, on June 29, 1913. His mother died when he was four, and he had almost no memories of her. Pete, as he was sometimes called, attended local schools and grew up in Athens.

Nelson "Petie" Seagraves standing in front of the Seagraves' house on Georgia Drive

He served as a medic in the U.S. Army during WWII and was stationed in Germany. Pete worked in the dye room at Climax Hosiery Mill for about 30 years. After the mill closed, he had several jobs over the years and later owned and operated Pete Seagraves' Service Station on Oconee Street.

Pete and Annie D had three children: William Harvey "Billy" Seagraves, Mary Ethelyn Seagraves Fields and Phillip Nelson

Seagraves. Known for his friendly, outgoing personality, Pete loved to eat, especially Annie D's biscuits. He died October 18, 1995, in a veteran's hospital in Augusta, Georgia, and is buried in Oconee Hill Cemetery next to Annie D and near his mother, Julia.

Harold Lee Seagraves

Harold Lee Seagraves and oldest son Bobby Seagraves—From Freddy Seagraves

Harold Seagraves, born April 17, 1917, was the youngest child of Harvey Lee "Bob" and Julia Suddeth Seagraves. After his mother died, when Harold was only about a year and a half old, he lived at the Peter Street Seagraves homeplace with his aunt Clela and uncle Fid.

Harold attended local schools and served on the USS JRY Blakely battleship during WWII. He joined the City of Athens Police Department and rose through the ranks to become a lieutenant. He also worked for the Clarke County Sheriff's Department.

Harold married Mary Fred Warwick, and they were the parents of Bobby Seagraves, who died on December 15, 1998, Freddy Seagraves, Lisa Seagraves Layne and Lynn Seagraves, who died on December 11, 2006. Harold died on April 19, 1966, at age 49 and is buried in Oconee Hill Cemetery.

The four youngest Seagraves children. Front row, L-R: Rebecca Seagraves Baugh, Barbara Seagraves Tiller Carter. Back row, L-R: David Seagraves, Donald Seagraves.

Susie Rebecca Seagraves Baugh

Rebecca Seagraves Baugh —From Freddy Seagraves

Rebecca Seagraves Baugh, born September 15, 1924, was the oldest daughter of Harvey Lee "Bob" and Reba Winn Seagraves. She became an avid reader at an early age, attended local schools, and earned multiple degrees at the University of Georgia. After teaching in schools in Granville, Marietta, and Athens High School, Rebecca served as a guidance counselor for the Clarke County School System. Rebecca taught Sunday School for various ages and groups, served on many committees, and sang in the East Athens Baptist Church choir.

Front row, L-R: Rebecca Seagraves Baugh, Herman Baugh, Barbara Seagraves Tiller Carter. Back row, L-R: David Seagraves, Trixie Williams Seagraves, Donald Seagraves, Melissa Hawkins Seagraves—From Pati Tiller Montgomery

Rebecca married fellow teacher Herman Baugh, and they enjoyed 43 happy years of marriage. The couple never had biological children together, but by opening the doors of their home to hosts of nieces and nephews, college students, church family, international students and their families, missionaries, and a menagerie of dogs and cats, they instilled a lot of love, faith, and wisdom into future generations. Rebecca died July 3, 2018, at age 93 and is buried in Oconee Hill Cemetery.

Barbara Anne Seagraves Tiller Carter

From L-R: Goss Tiller, Barbara Seagraves Tiller Carter, daughters Becky Tiller Harrison, Beth Tiller Umbarger and Pati Tiller Montgomery

Barbara Seagraves Tiller Carter, born October 21, 1926, was the youngest daughter of Harvey Lee "Bob" and Reba Winn Seagraves.

She attended local schools and studied at Tift College in Forsyth, Georgia, later earning advanced degrees from the Universities of Georgia and Alabama. Barbara taught mathematics for 38 years at schools that included Bradley County High School and Lee College (now Lee University) in Cleveland, Tennessee, and eventually became both teacher and vice-principal at Cleveland Day School, which she helped to found.

In 1970, Barbara and her family moved to Oxford, Alabama, where Barbara began teaching at the Donoho School (then the Anniston Academy). She served as Math Department Head at the Donoho School until 1988, when she became Computer Department Head, and held that position until she retired at the close of the 1991 school year.

Front row, Rebecca Seagraves Baugh. Back row, Pati Tiller Montgomery with her mother Barbara Seagraves Tiller Carter—From Pati Tiller Montgomery

During retirement, Barbara remained active at Meadowbrook Baptist Church, maintained her membership in Delta Kappa Gamma, and joined the Golden "K" Kiwanis Club and the local Daughters of the American Revolution.

Barbara's first husband, Goss Tiller, died unexpectedly in 1976. She and Goss were the parents of Anne Rebecca Tiller Harrison, Barbara Elizabeth Tiller Umbarger and Pati Tiller Montgomery. After living for many years as a widow, Barbara married (ret) Col. Bryant E. Carter and became stepmother to his daughter Mettie Bell. Barbara died on March 16, 2019, and is buried in Alabama.

Donald Winn Seagraves, Sr.

Donald Winn Seagraves, Sr., a Shriner, riding in a long ago Winterville Marigold Festival parade—Photo by Donny Bailey Seagraves

Donald Seagraves, born September 2, 1930, was the oldest son of Harvey Lee "Bob" and Reba Winn Seagraves. He attended local schools, including Athens High School, where he lettered in football, basketball and baseball. For many years, he proudly carried a clipping in his wallet from the *New York Sun-Times* about his unassisted triple play in an Athens High School baseball game.

Front row: Rebecca Seagraves Baugh, Donald Winn Seagraves. Back row: David Hartford Seagraves, Barbara Seagraves Tiller Carter.—From Pati Tiller Montgomery

Donald's love of the Georgia Bulldogs was legendary. A long-time season ticket holder, he rarely missed a game. He was a veteran of the U.S. Air Force and the Reserves and a member of the Masons and the Shriners. He had a long and distinguished career in the real estate division of the U.S. Army Corps of Engineers and worked on projects in Georgia, Alabama and Mississippi. After retiring, Donald was a consultant for the Corps and later became a tax assessor in Elberton, Georgia.

Donald married Melissa Hawkins, and they were the parents of Donald Winn "Donnie" Seagraves, Jr., who died in 2017, and Hope Seagraves Austin. Donald Sr. died on February 25, 2015, and is buried in Oconee Hill Cemetery.

David Hartford Seagraves

L-R: David Seagraves, Donald Seagraves, unknown—From Hope Seagraves Austin

Harvey Lee "Bob" and Reba Winn Seagraves' youngest son, David Hartford Seagraves, graduated from Clemson University with a Bachelor of Science degree in Textile Manufacturing. He worked at the Athens Chicopee Mill for eighteen years, rising to plant superintendent, later serving as plant manager of the Crompton Textile Company, and Executive Vice President of the Alabama Textile Manufacturers Association.

Like his father, Bob, David served as an Athens First Ward Councilmember, as Mayor Pro-tem, and as chairperson of the Model

Cities Policy Board. He also served on the Clarke County Board of Education. David's military service in the U.S. Navy included time as an officer aboard the USS Everglades.

David married Trixie Williams, and they are the parents of Lacy Seagraves Boatfield and David "Skipper" Seagraves, Jr. At the time this book was written, David, Sr. was the only child of Harvey Lee "Bob" Seagraves still living.[3]

David and Trixie Williams Seagraves in 1996

Seagraves siblings, their spouses and a first cousin gathered at a long ago Farr - Seagraves family reunion, hosted by J.B. Farr. Front row, L-R: Gaynelle Seagraves Farr Wansley, Nelson "Petie" Seagraves, Rebecca Seagraves Baugh, Barbara Seagraves Tiller Carter, Donald Seagraves, David Seagraves. Back row, L-R: Dick Wansley, Anne "Annie D" Seagraves, Bessie Seagraves Kemp (daughter of Charles "Hard Charlie" Seagraves), Herman Baugh, Sarah James Seagraves (widow of Frank Ed Seagraves), Melissa Hawkins Seagraves, Trixie Williams Seagraves.—From Hope Seagraves Austin

Chapter 13

Public Safety

Many of Hardy and Pink Seagraves' descendants have served the City of Athens Police Department, including sons Charles "Hard Charlie" Seagraves as chief of police, Fred "Shack" Seagraves as police department captain and chief of detectives, and grandsons Frank Ed Seagraves, who was a captain in the City of Athens Police Department, and Harold Seagraves, an Athens Police Department lieutenant who also worked for the Clarke County Sheriff's Department. Albert D. "Strut" Seagraves, son of Police Chief "Hard Charlie" Seagraves, worked for the Clarke County Sheriff's department.

In Madison County, Georgia, several Seagraves worked in law enforcement, including Josiah Milsey Seagraves and his grandson Weyman Seagraves, who served as a Madison County Sheriff's deputy under Sheriff Jack Fortson. Another Seagraves who worked in public safety was Madison County's longtime sheriff Dewey Seagraves.

Josiah's son, Arthur Ford Seagraves, Weyman Seagraves' father, was only 5' 2" tall and was too short to work as a police officer or sheriff's deputy, according to his grandson John Seagraves.

"But Ford was tall enough to serve two terms in the Georgia Senate and two terms in the Georgia House of Representatives in the 1940s," John said.

Many Hansfords descended from Hardy and Pink Seagraves and their daughter, Lula Armenia Seagraves Hansford and her husband Mark C. Hansford, also worked in law enforcement, including Allen T. Hansford, Edward C. Hansford, James M. Hansford, and Mark Ed Hansford.

Charles Emory "Hard Charlie" Seagraves

Charles Emory "Hard Charlie" Seagraves, a City of Athens police chief. This photo is from the early 1930s.—From Hope Seagraves Austin

Charles Emory "Hard Charlie" (sometimes spelled "Charley") Seagraves, oldest son of Hardy and Pink Carithers Seagraves, was born November 19, 1877, in Athens, Georgia. He was a brother to

Bessie (who died young), Harvey Lee "Bob," Edward Pope "Fid," Frederick "Shack," Lula, Clela and Leonard "Len."

His U.S. World War I draft registration card says Charlie was stout and of medium height. His hair color was brown (at that time — it turned white early, a common Seagraves family trait), and his eyes were brown.

Captain of Police Charles "Hard Charlie" Seagraves, Athens, Georgia—From The Police Review, 1926

Charles married twice. First wife, Mary E. Bullock, died at age 22, leaving behind their son, Carl Seagraves. His second wife was Alton "Alti" Ethel Richards. They were the parents of Gilbert G. Seagraves, Bessie Seagraves Kemp, Charles Emory Seagraves, Jr., who died when he was only six years old, Edna Louise Seagraves, who was the first manager of the Athens Area Food Bank in 1981, Albert D. "Strut" Seagraves, who also worked in law enforcement, Ralph Donald Seagraves and Wallace Leroy Seagraves.

Charles joined the City of Athens Police Department as a young man and rose through the ranks to become captain of detectives and then, near the end of his career, chief of police.

In a 1926 article in *The Police Review*, Seagraves (a captain of police at the time) said: "I have never had to use my gun, although my arrests have been many and the people I dealt with often of desperate character. I have found, furthermore, that there is scarcely ever any actual necessity of using a gun except as a last resort. Time has proven to me that for the officer to remain cool and to use fair and square methods with his prisoner is by far the best system."[1]

Family legend says this gun, from the collection of the late Harvey Hill "Sleepy" Seagraves, once belonged to Police Chief Charles "Hard Charlie" Seagraves, Sleepy's uncle. —Photo by Donny Bailey Seagraves

Habitual criminals who found him hard to evade when they were up to no good gave Hard Charlie his nickname during his eighteen years as chief of the Athens detective force. No matter where they went in Athens, Hard Charlie always found them, sometimes jumping out from behind bushes to arrest them, according to his daughter Bessie Seagraves Kemp. Some say Charlie didn't carry a gun. Charlie himself said he had never had to use his gun in the line of duty.[2]

Early Police Force

City of Athens, Georgia early police force in 1906. Charles Emory "Hard Charlie" Seagraves is on the second row, second from the right. On the top row, his brother, Fred "Shack" Seagraves may be second from the left.—From Athens, Georgia: Home of the University of Georgia 1801 - 1951

In an undated newspaper clipping found in Anne Seagraves'

papers and entitled: "From Sanford's Scrapbook" by Dr. Shelton Sanford as told to Bob Tritt Jr., Dr. Sanford tells a story about an absentminded professor who received a telegram from a not-too-distant city saying, "Send $200 c/o Western Union. Waive identification. (Signed) Junior."

This vintage photo, most likely circa 1920, was found in a trunk that came from the Seagraves' homeplace on Peter Street. The law enforcement officers and the gentleman in the middle are unidentified, but the officer on the left might be Charles Emory "Hard Charlie" Seagraves, or another officer from that time, and the officer on the right may be Frederick "Shack" Seagraves or, if this is a later photo, Harold Seagraves. Freddy Seagraves suggested that the officer on the right might be his late father, Harold Seagraves, but the dates don't seem to work out. Harold was born in 1917. This photo may have been part of an Athens Police Department fundraising drive.—From Freddy Seagraves

Back in those days, a college professor could not easily dig up $200 for bail regardless of what problem his son was having, Dr. Sanford said. So this gentleman went immediately to City Hall to consult with the police chief.

The chief, known affectionately to his clientele as "Hard Charlie," said, "Let me handle this."

Hard Charlie immediately called his counterpart in said city and said, "Have you got Junior?"

"Yes," was the reply.

"Hold him. He is wanted in Athens. I'm sending for him."

Dr. Sanford continued, "Hard Charlie then sent a neatly uniformed police officer wearing a new patent leather visored cap to retrieve the miscreant and restore him to the tender loving care of his parents."

Charles E. "Hard Charlie" Seagraves died on October 4, 1934, while serving as Athens police chief, and is buried in Oconee Hill Cemetery. His obituary in the *Atlanta Constitution* said he solved many crimes during his Athens Police Department career, including those of local and national importance.

Frederick "Shack" Seagraves

Fred "Shack" Seagraves was born February 12, 1880, in Athens, Georgia. He was a son of Hardy and Pink Seagraves and a brother to Charles "Hard Charlie," Harvey Lee "Bob," Bessie, Edward Pope "Fid," Lula, Clela and Leonard "Len."

Fred attended local schools. His WWI Draft Registration card lists his physical build as stout, his height as medium, his hair as gray (like many Seagraves, his hair grayed early and eventually turned white), and his eye color as brown. In the early 1900s, Fred went to work for the City of Athens Police Department and rose through the ranks to become captain of detectives.

Captain of Police Detectives Fred "Shack" Seagraves, who was a brother of City of Athens Police Department Chief Charles Emory "Hard Charlie" Seagraves—From The Police Review, 1926

Fred married Maud Cook Watson, widow of former City of Athens Fire Chief Doma Watson, Sr., November 29, 1932, when he was 51 and became a stepdad to her children, Doma, Jr., Ethel, and Dorita. In a 1940 U. S. Federal Census record, he is listed as Fred Senoranes (Fred Seagraves), age 60, living at 359 Hancock Avenue. He owned this house, and its value was $2,700 (about $55,447.20 in today's dollars). He is a captain in government with a yearly salary of $1,620 (about $32,857.60 in today's dollars). Captain Seagraves' house was demolished many years ago, and the place where it once stood was a parking lot at the time this book was written.

Captain Fred "Shack" Seagraves' tombstone in Oconee Hill Cemetery—Photo by Donny Bailey Seagraves

In an article from a 1926 edition of *The Police Review*, the unidentified writer says there is a certain atmosphere of strength in the face of Captain Seagraves, which also is reflected in the work he does. The article goes on to say, "Captain Seagraves is a strong man. Not merely in a physical sense, although he is that also, but in a moral sense. He will tolerate no departure from the strict code of moral ethics, either in others or in himself. He clings always to that which is right, doing his work in an honest and conscientious manner and living the life of a valuable and worthwhile citizen."

Fred died on March 21, 1950 and is buried in Oconee Hill Cemetery. His obituary said that FBI Director J. Edgar Hoover once cited him. We do not know what Fred was cited for, but we can guess that it might have been his outstanding record of solving numerous local and national crimes during his long public safety career.

Juddie Bernard Farr, Sr.

Juddie Bernard Farr, Sr. served in the Athens Police Department and the Athens Fire Department. He was the first husband of Gaynelle Seagraves Farr Wansley.—Photo from The Police Review

A 1926 article in *The Police Review* begins, "Farr is bound to go far in the police business. He has already gone far. While he is listed as a patrolman, he has traveled far in the knowledge he has acquired concerning the work and far in the esteem of his superiors and fellow officers. Since coming to the Athens department on October 9, 1924, Farr has shown steady progress in the work."

Juddie Bernard "J. B." Farr, Sr. was only 21 years old when his profile as an up-and-coming police officer appeared in *The Police Review*. He eventually went to work for the Athens Fire Department, rising through the ranks to become assistant chief of engine one at station one on Thomas Street.

Unfortunately, his career there was cut short by a tragic fire truck accident. In the book, *Across The River: The People, Places, and Culture of East Athens* by Maxine Pinson Easom and Patsy Hawkins Arnold, Gary Doster says Assistant Chief Farr was killed on duty

December 20, 1937, when he and several other firefighters were riding in a 1921 American LaFrance fire truck, rushing to the scene of a grass fire on Lumpkin Street.

J. B. Farr was survived by his wife, Gaynelle Seagraves Farr Wansley, and their two children, Julia Farr DeRose Holzworth and Judd Farr, Jr. He is buried in Oconee Hill Cemetery.

Harold Lee Seagraves

Clarke County Police Force

This 1950s photo is of the Clarke County Police Force. Pictured (seated, L-R) are: the late J.W. Whitehead, Capt. George Farmer, the late Lt. Harold Seagraves, Lt. Walt Milner.

Standing (L-R) are: the late Lt. Mack Childers, the late Albert "Strut" Seagraves, Lt Paul Wages, Frank Burger. This was the first Clarke County Police Force.

This 1950s photo of the first Clarke County Police Force includes Harold Seagraves, front row third from the left and Albert "Strut" Seagraves back row, second from the left.— From undated Athens Banner Herald - Athens Daily News Classic Scene Sunday Magazine clipping.

Harold Seagraves, youngest son of Harvey Lee "Bob" and Julia Suddeth Seagraves, served in both the City of Athens Police Department and the Clarke County Sheriff's Department. You can read more about Harold in chapter 12.

Frank Edward Seagraves

Captain Frank Ed Seagraves—From Missy Seagraves Jackson

Frank Ed Seagraves served in the City of Athens Police Department, rising to the rank of captain. You can read more about him in chapter 12.

James "Jimmy" Hansford

Jimmy Hansford, Hardy and Pink Seagraves' great-grandson, Mark C. and Lula Seagraves Hansford's grandson and a son of Ed and Velma Hansford, worked his way up through the City of Athens Fire Department to become Athens fire chief. He later served as state fire marshall and was head of the Georgia Public Training Center in Forsyth, Georgia during his long and distinguished career in public safety.

James "Jimmy" Hansford, former City of Athens fire chief—From Jimmy Hansford

Phillip Nelson Seagraves

Phillip Seagraves, Nelson "Petie" and Anne "Annie D" Seagraves' youngest son, stands on top of Athens City Hall as he inspects the brass eagle while working for the Athens Clarke County Unified Government.

Hardy and Pink's great-grandson Phillip Seagraves, grandson of Harvey Lee "Bob" and Julia Suddeth Seagraves and youngest son of Annie D and Nelson "Petie" Seagraves, worked for the City of Athens, Clarke County, and the Athens-Clarke County Unified Government for 27 years, retiring as assistant director of the Building Permits and Inspections Department, which exists to protect the public's health, safety and general welfare.

Many Seagraves and Pettyjohn family members served in the military. Here are a few family military photos. Bottom row, L-R: Center back row Nelson "Petie" Seagraves; Victor "Vic" Pettyjohn; back row fourth from the left Phillip Seagraves. Top row, L-R: Nelson "Petie" Seagraves; James "Jimmy" Hansford; back row right Harold Seagraves.

Chapter 14

Side Dishes

Sandra Jo "Sandy" Seagraves' Memories

Sandy Seagraves, youngest daughter of Billy and Jo Dobbins Seagraves, granddaughter of Nelson "Petie" and Annie D Seagraves and great-granddaughter of Harvey Lee "Bob" and Julia Suddeth Seagraves, has many special memories of her Seagraves' grandparents' house on Georgia Drive.

"When I was a little girl, my grandmother always made what she called "baby biscuits" for me with a special glass that cut them out small. Her biscuits were the best I've ever tasted," Sandy said.

Sandy's other favorite meal that her grandmother Annie D cooked for her when she visited was country ham and redeye gravy.

"I can still taste her redeye gravy — it was so delicious. I especially enjoyed going to my grandparents' house at Christmas. Grandmother Anne would have wedding cookies, divinity and fudge, all scratch-made and in that 3-tiered compote.

Sandy Seagraves and older sister Suzanne Seagraves Gerling at their grandparents' house on Georgia Drive during a long ago Christmas visit. In the background, to the right, are their grandmother Anne's "choir people decorations," made from old telephone books.

"My grandmother's kitchen in the house on Georgia Drive was everything. It was always buzzing with laughter, delicious food smells, and penny poker around the kitchen table at night."

Sandy Seagraves, with her mother, Jo, playing penny poker in grandmother Annie D's kitchen.

Beer Batter Onions

- *1 1/2 cups all-purpose flour*
- *1 teaspoon salt*
- *1 1/2 cups beer*
- *3 large onions cut into 1/2-inch slices*
- *Hot salad oil*
- *Salt to taste*

Combine flour and salt. Stir in beer and beat until smooth. Let batter stand for three hours. Separate onion slices into rings. Dip in batter and fry in two inches of hot salad oil at 375 degrees until golden brown. Sprinkle with salt.—*Anne Seagraves, Clarke County, Georgia*

Sandy Seagraves graduated from the University of Georgia school of drama and once worked as a model in New York.—From Sandy Seagraves

Ethel Pettyjohn's Canned Green Beans

- *1 cup vinegar to a dishpan full of fresh, uncooked green beans*

- *1 cup sugar*

Bring beans to a boil and boil twenty minutes. Put beans in sterilized jars. Put a tablespoon of salt to one quart of beans and then seal up.—Ethel Strickland Pettyjohn, Clarke County, Georgia.[1]

An antique canning jar from Ethel Pettyjohn's kitchen in the former Pettyjohn house on Boulevard—Photo by Donny Bailey Seagraves

Cornbread Dressing

- *2 cups cornmeal mix*
- *2 cups buttermilk*
- *2 eggs*

Mix the above in a large metal bowl. Put 1/2 cup of Crisco in iron skillet. Put skillet with Crisco in cold oven, then set the oven to 450 degrees and let the Crisco melt. It takes about ten minutes while the oven heats. Watch it closely and take skillet out of oven as soon as shortening melts. (It could catch on fire if you don't remove the skillet as soon as shortening melts.)

Jodie Locklear and Jen Seagraves wearing their favorite aprons—From Jen Seagraves

Cut up two stalks of celery and one onion (I like sweet onions). Saute onion in about three or four tablespoons of olive oil in skillet (not the one with the Crisco. You should have taken that one out of the oven by now, or you'll need to call the fire department.) Set aside sautéed onion and celery.

Take iron skillet with melted shortening and move in a motion that causes melted shortening to swirl around inside the skillet and coat the sides. Then pour about half of the melted shortening into the metal bowl where you have the cornmeal mixture. Mix well, then pour into iron skillet and bake at 450 degrees for about twenty minutes, until almost done (if making cornbread instead of dressing, bake twenty-five minutes, then eat).

After cornbread cools, crumble it in a bowl and add two cans low-fat chicken broth, two eggs, about one-half teaspoon sage, about a tablespoon of salt, some pepper to taste. Mix all together, put in greased or sprayed pan or oven-proof glass casserole dish and bake about forty-five minutes to an hour, or until brown and set into the consistency you like. Enjoy!—*Donny Bailey Seagraves, Clarke County, Georgia*

Andrew Mathew "Andy" Seagraves

Andrew Mathew "Andy" Seagraves, fraternal twin brother of Hardy Calloway Seagraves—From Kay Thomas, Andrew Mathew "Andy" and Emaline Seagraves' great-granddaughter

By the time the 1912 *Athens City Directory* was published, Hardy Seagraves' fraternal twin brother, Andrew Mathew "Andy"

Seagraves, lived at 824 Oconee Street, and his occupation was fireman. He later lived in two other houses in the same neighborhood.

Andy and his wife, Martha Emaline Peeler, had daughters: Ella F. (1877 - 1944), Mary Elizabeth "Lizzie" (1878 - 1925), Maude K. (1883 - 1947), Emma Estelle (1887 - 1983), Minnie Odelle (1889 - 1961) and Annie Evelyn (1893 - 1969).

One of Andy and Emaline Seagraves' houses on Oconee Street in East Athens, Georgia. They also lived in two other houses in the same East Athens neighborhood.—Photo by Donny Bailey Seagraves

On an unknown date, Emaline gave birth to twins, Lonie and Johnnie, who apparently died at or shortly after birth, and share a tombstone with two hearts in Oconee Hill Cemetery near their parents' graves.

Double heart headstone of Segraves (Seagraves) twins Johnnie and Lonie, near their parents' graves in Oconee Hill Cemetery—From Kay Thomas, great-granddaughter of Andrew Mathew "Andy" Seagraves

On Johnnie's tombstone heart, the inscription reads, "A Little Bud of Love To Bloom With God Above." We do not know if Johnnie was a son or a daughter since the name "Johnnie" can be a boy's or a girl's name. The inscription on Lonie's tombstone heart reads, "How Much of Light, How Much of Joy is Burried With a Darling Boy."

Though Andy and Emaline Seagraves most assuredly loved and cherished their many daughters, their hearts must have been broken when they lost their twins.

Brenda Seagraves

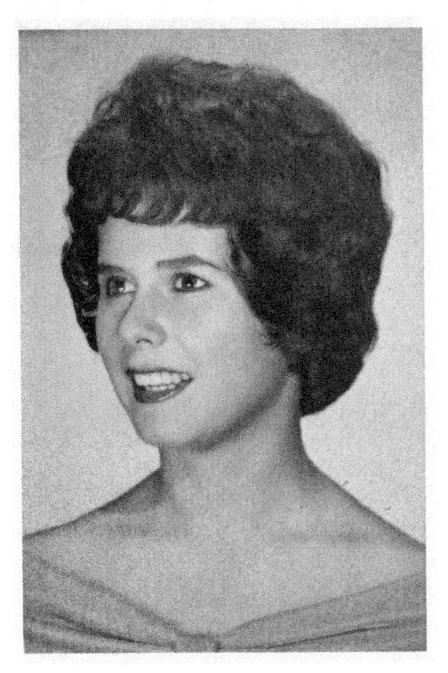

Brenda Seagraves, a former Miss UGA and Miss USA Pageant contestant—From Brenda Seagraves

Hardy and Pink's great-granddaughter, Brenda Seagraves, attended the University of Georgia. She was crowned Miss UGA in 1965 and competed in the Miss USA Pageant. Brenda, a longtime teacher, is the granddaughter of Leonard "Len" and Annie Lou Seagraves and daughter of James Leonard "Tensie" and Mary Ruth Seagraves.

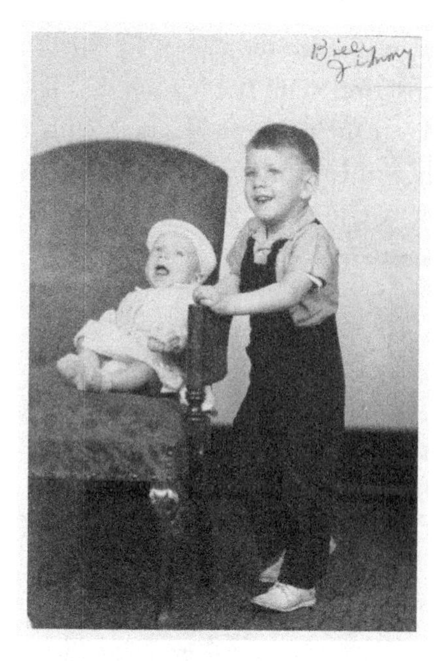

Billy and Jimmy Hansford, sons of Ed and Velma Hansford, grandsons of Mark C. and Lula Hansford, and great-grandsons of Hardy and Pink Seagraves.

Old Fashioned Stewed Tomatoes

- *2 slices bread*
- *2 tablespoons butter*
- *1 large can tomatoes*
- *1 tablespoon sugar*
- *Salt and pepper*

Cut bread into cubes. Brown lightly in butter. Add remaining ingredients and simmer gently until thoroughly heated. Makes six one-half cup servings.—*Anne Seagraves, Clarke County, Georgia*

Seagraves cousins, L-R: Hope Seagraves Austin, Becky Tiller Harrison, Beth Tiller Umbarger, Pati Tiller Montgomery, Lacey Seagraves Boatfield.—From Pati Tiller Montgomery

Corn Pudding

- *2 cans creamed corn*
- *1 can whole kernel corn*
- *3 eggs, beaten*
- *1 tablespoon sugar*
- *1 teaspoon salt*
- *1/3 cup melted margarine*
- *1/2 cup grated cheese*
- *1/3 cup finely chopped onion*
- *1/3 cup finely chopped green pepper*
- *1 1/3 cup milk*
- *4 heaping tablespoons flour*

Mix corn, eggs, sugar, salt, margarine, cheese, onions, green pepper. Put the milk in a pint glass jar. Add the flour. Put lid on and shake vigorously until flour is well blended. Add to corn mixture and blend well. Pour into a nine-by-thirteen-inch casserole dish. Dribble two tablespoons melted margarine on top, and add two tablespoons grated cheese over the top. Bake at 350 degrees for one hour. —*Ann Seagraves, Madison County, Georgia*

Harold Seagraves—From Freddy Seagraves

Corn Pudding Casserole

In a large mixing bowl, mix the following:

- *2 cans creamed corn*
- *1 can "drained" kernel corn*
- *3 eggs, beaten*
- *1 tablespoon sugar*
- *1 teaspoon salt*
- *Black pepper as desired*
- *1/3 cup MELTED margarine (Save some melted margarine to pour on top before sprinkling on the grated cheese.)*
- *1/2 cup coarsely grated cheese (suggest mild cheddar)*
- *1/3 cup finely chopped Vidalia onion*
- *1/3 cup finely chopped bell pepper*
- *Your choice: Add finely chopped pimento (for accent color)*

Into a (pint-sized glass jar), mix one and one-third cups of milk and add four heaping tablespoons of flour. Put the lid on tightly and shake vigorously until flour is well blended. Then add flour/milk mixture to the above ingredients in the large mixing bowl.

Prepare your nine-by-thirteen-inch glass casserole dish by spraying with Pam. A clear glass casserole dish is recommended. Dribble a little melted margarine on top, add several tablespoons of grated cheese, and spread evenly over the casserole. Bake at 350 degrees for approximately one hour or until golden brown.—*Ann Seagraves, Madison County, Georgia*

Susan DeRose and the OK Cafe

The OK Cafe in Atlanta, Georgia—Photo by Tim Younkers

Susan DeRose, Hardy and Pink's great-great-granddaughter, granddaughter of Judd Farr, Sr. and Gaynelle Seagraves Farr Wansley, and daughter of Michael DeRose and Julia Farr DeRose Holtzworth, attended the University of Georgia and learned to appreciate delicious Southern food from an early age in her grandmother Gaynelle's Five Points Athens kitchen.

In 1987, Susan and partner Richard Lewis opened The Ok Cafe in Atlanta and it quickly became so popular that crowds stood in line to get in. According to Susan, Richard and the team at OK Cafe, people come to the cafe for quality food and "the sort of menu your grandmother might have made for Sunday dinner."

A first edition dust jacket from the novel To Kill A Mockingbird by Harper Lee

If the restaurant name sounds familiar, that's because the OK Cafe was named as a tribute to a place mentioned in Harper Lee's famous book *To Kill a Mockingbird.* A few years ago, when I was a member of the Atlanta Chapter of author Rosemary Danielle's Zona Rosa writers' group, several of us would stop at the OK Cafe on our way to the monthly meetings. Besides the delicious Southern food (very inspirational for our writing), we enjoyed admiring the autographed copy of Harper Lee's *To Kill a Mockingbird* as we walked into the main entrance hallway to find a seat.

Many publications, including *Money*, *Forbes*, *Southern Living* and *Ladies Home Journal*, have praised the OK Cafe, one of three restaurants owned and operated by Susan and Richard's Liberty House Restaurant Corporation. Their other two restaurants, Bones and the Blue Ridge Grill, also have garnered rave reviews.

Besides being a well-known and successful restaurateur, Susan is a screenwriter and producer of the feature film, *Charming the Hearts of Men*, which stars Kelsey Grammer, Anna Friel and Sean Astin. This well-reviewed movie opened in theaters and became available for streaming on AppleTV+ and Amazon in 2021.—*Donny Bailey Seagraves* [2]

Great Macaroni and Cheese

Macaroni and Cheese—Photo by Donny Bailey Seagraves

- *Cook 2 cups macaroni according to package directions*
- *Drain and add 1 stick margarine*
- *Salt to taste*
- *2 eggs (beaten)*
- *1/2 cup to 1 cup sweet milk (it needs to be soupy)*
- *12-ounce (grated) sharp cheese*

Mix all together and pour into greased baking dish. Sprinkle some grated cheese on top. Bake at 400 degrees for about thirty minutes or until bubbly.—*Anne Seagraves, Clarke County, Georgia*

"My uncle, Harold Seagraves, died a few days before he would have celebrated his fiftieth birthday. Many other Seagraves died in their fifties and sixties, and they all liked to eat. My dad, Nelson "Petie" Seagraves, used to say, 'Give a Seagraves a fork and he'll dig his own grave.' Petie ate his share of high-fat Southern food and about a million of Annie D's biscuits, but somehow he lived to 82."

— Phillip Seagraves

Macaroni and Cheese

- *1 pound macaroni elbows or shells or penne pasta*
- *8 ounces shredded sharp cheddar cheese*
- *8 ounces shredded mild cheddar cheese*
- *About 6 ounces (more or less, your preference) shredded cheddar and Monterey jack cheese (or whatever kind of cheese you like best)*
- *1/2 stick butter (can use margarine to reduce fat)*
- *About 6 tablespoons of flour (more or less, depending on how thick you want the sauce)*
- *4 cups milk (to reduce fat, you could use 2%)*

Boil the pasta using directions on box. Drain. In a large pot, melt butter, then add flour and milk. Stir over low heat until mixture thickens. Turn off heat and add the shredded sharp cheddar and the mild cheddar. Stir until cheese has melted and you have a cheese sauce. Add the pasta and mix well. Pour into a large thirteen-by-nine-inch oven-safe glass casserole dish or pan. Sprinkle the shredded cheddar and Monterey jack cheese over the top of the mac and cheese.

Bake in a 350-degree oven for thirty minutes or until browned on top. Let cool on stovetop, then serve with your favorite green vegetable or salad. Great leftover and freezes well.—*Donny Bailey Seagraves, Clarke County, Georgia*

Hot Pimiento Cheese

- *1 pound processed American cheese (shredded)*
- *1/4 cup tomato sauce*
- *1 tablespoon hot sauce*
- *1/2 cup mayonnaise*
- *3/4 cup (drained) diced pimiento*

Combine first four ingredients (stir well). Fold in pimiento. Cover and chill thoroughly. Yields three and one-third cups.—*Anne Seagraves, Clarke County, Georgia*

Hope Seagraves Austin with her brother Donald Winn "Donnie" Seagraves, Jr., who died in 2017. Hope and her brother are the children of Donald Winn and Melissa Hawkins Seagraves, grandchildren of Harvey Lee "Bob" and Reba Winn Seagraves, and great-grandchildren of Hardy and Pink Carithers Seagraves. —From Hope Austin Seagraves

Onion Casserole

- *1 (15 ounce) can whole shoe peg corn*
- *1 (15-ounce) can of French-style green beans*
- *1 can cream of celery soup*
- *1/2 cup grated cheese*
- *1/2 cup chopped onions*
- *1/2 cup sour cream*
- *1 stick margarine, melted*
- *36 Ritz crackers, crumbled*

Mix corn, drained, and green beans with a little salt and pepper. Spread into greased casserole dish. Mix soup, cheese, onions and sour cream. Put crushed crackers on top, and then pour melted margarine over top. Bake at 350 degrees for about forty-five minutes.—*Anne Seagraves, Clarke County, Georgia*

Annie D Seagraves

Potato Balls Fried Crisp

- *2 cups (cooked) mashed potatoes packed in cup*
- *1/4 cup grated cheese*
- *2 tablespoons low-fat cottage cheese*
- *1 large egg*
- *Salt and pepper to taste*
- *All-purpose flour*

Stir the potatoes, cheese, cottage cheese, egg, salt and pepper well. I use two large spoons to shape mixture into one-and-one-half-inch balls. Roll lightly in flour. Fry in deep hot fat at 375 degrees until golden brown. Serve at once.—*Anne Seagraves, Clarke County, Georgia*

~

Nelson Hardy "Petie" Seagraves with his fraternal twin grandchildren Jen and Greg Seagraves—Photo by Donny Bailey Seagraves

Twins in the Family

Fraternal twins run in both the Seagraves and Pettyjohn families. On the Seagraves side, fraternal twins Hardy and Andrew "Andy" Seagraves, who were born in Madison County, Georgia, were some of the first Seagraves to move to Athens-Clarke County, Georgia.

Matthew Nash and Andrew Nath Austin, fraternal twin sons of Wayne and Hope Seagraves Austin. Nath passed away in 1981.—From Hope Seagraves Austin

Andy and his wife Emaline had one set of twins, Johnnie and Lonie, that we know of, who died at or soon after birth.

Austin and Taylor Loden, fraternal twin son and daughter of Gary and Lori Fields Loden

There are several sets of fraternal twins among Hardy and Pink Seagraves' descendants, including son Harvey Bob Seagraves' twin great-grandchildren: Jennifer "Jen" and Gregory "Greg" Seagraves, Matthew Nash and Andrew Nath Austin, Nancy and Amy Farr and twin great-great-grandchildren Austin and Taylor Loden.

Fraternal twins William and Henry Pettyjohn

On the Pettyjohn side, William and Henry Pettyjohn were fraternal twins. We do not know of other fraternal twins in that part of the family, but we wouldn't be surprised if there were many more.

Scalloped Tomatoes

Harold Lee and Mary Fred Warwick Seagraves

- *1 - 2 cans or 2 1/2 cups cooked tomatoes*
- *2 tablespoons chopped onion*
- *1 1/4 teaspoon salt*
- *2 tablespoons butter*
- *Dash black pepper*
- *2 tablespoons sugar*
- *1 cup soft bread crumbs*

Preheat oven to 400 degrees. Grease a baking dish. Combine tomatoes, onion, salt, pepper and sugar. Pour into baking dish and dot with butter. Top the bread crumbs with butter. (Put bread crumbs over tomato mixture). Bake in hot oven for twenty-five minutes or until brown.—*Anne Seagraves, Clarke County, Georgia*

Squash Casserole

- *2 cups mashed squash (cooked)*
- *1/2 cup grated cheese*
- *1 cup crushed crackers (Ritz)*
- *2 eggs*
- *1 small chopped onion*
- *1/2 cup sweet milk*

Mix well. Put in buttered casserole dish. Top with a few cracker crumbs and bake at 325 degrees for forty-five minutes.—*Anne Seagraves, Clarke County, Georgia*

This cast-iron pot came from Will and Ethel Pettyjohn's house on Boulevard. The family may have brought this pot with them when they moved to Athens or might have purchased it in Athens after they arrived. Annie D cooked fresh green beans and other vegetables in this pot.—Photo by Donny Bailey Seagraves

Squash Casserole – Another Version

- *2 1/2 cups cooked squash (mashed)*
- *1 can cream of chicken soup*
- *1 cup sour cream*
- *1 grated squash*
- *2 tablespoons grated onion*
- *1 small jar pimento (chopped)*
- *Herb-seasoned stuffing mix.*

Mix all ingredients except stuffing mix. Put in casserole dish. Sprinkle stuffing mix on top. Bake at 350 degrees for about thirty minutes.—*Anne Seagraves, Clarke County, Georgia*

Bottom row, L-R: Lori Fields Loden; Billy Seagraves; Carl Seagraves, oldest son of Charles E. "Hard Charlie" Seagraves with two young men who may be his brothers; Carl is in the middle. Top row, L-R: Sandy Seagraves modeling for a Just My Size advertising campaign; Billy Seagraves, Phillip Seagraves, Nelson "Petie" Seagraves; Phillip Seagraves with his older sister Mary Seagraves Fields.

Chapter 15

Cakes

Annie D's Neighbor "Miss" Della Huff

Back in the day, Annie D and Petie's Georgia Drive neighbors often stopped by to visit. One such neighbor was "Miss" Della Huff. Phillip and I would sometimes find her sitting in his parent's living room or at the kitchen table, eating some of Annie D's delicious food.

After she cleaned her plate, one of Della's favorite things to say was, "Darling, I done et all I can et."

Here's an article I wrote many years ago about "Miss" Della Huff for the *Athens-Banner Herald - Athens Daily News Classic Scene Sunday Magazine.*—Donny Bailey Seagraves

Meet "Miss" Della Huff, A Classic Athenian

Della Huff was born in Gwinnett County, Georgia, on the first day of September in 1894, but she can't remember living anywhere but Athens, Georgia.

"When I was a little girl, my father night-watched at the Foundry, and we lived in the Foundry house. I remember when the wagons came up Foundry Street, covered wagons, and we'd buy apples from them.

"Miss" Della Huff, Annie D's longtime neighbor

"And then we moved to the corner of Baxter and Newton Streets," Della continues. "We lived on Dubose Street, too. We used water out of a well back then, and I remember we had five washtubs on the porch to wash our clothes in."

After attending a private school at the "old Navy yard," Della dropped out of school to work when her mother became ill.

"I was a little bitty thing, maybe eight or nine or ten years old when I first started working in that factory down there on the river," she says, referring to the Athens Manufacturing Company building, which now houses (at the time this article was written) O'Malley's, a popular student hangout.

"Back then, it was just a cotton mill. They'd give children like me the easy jobs. I run spinning things. The sides were as long as this room, and I run six of them. We took big roping and wound it up, and it'd come down through the machinery and make a fine thread. I used to be so tired I'd lay down on the floor and go to sleep sometimes. It was hard work.

"Then I went over to the knitting mill," Miss Della says, pointing towards the spot down the hill to what once was the old Climax Hosiery Mill (and later the Stitchcraft sewing plant). "Mr. Dudley, he was a sweet thing. He said, 'Della, you won't stay here.' I just stayed forty years."

Mrs. Huff and her late husband, Craig, an Athens native who worked with his brothers at the old American Cafe, had three children. One daughter lives on Best Drive in Athens and the other one lives in Winder. "They killed my boy, Eugene," Della says sadly, holding up a faded baby picture. "Somebody in the hospital gave him the wrong shot."

Miss Della has lived a simple life during her many years in Athens. "We raised everything but our flour, sugar and coffee. I had a pig once that weighed 450 pounds. We laid him right out here and cut him up," she says, pointing to the hallway of her in-town East Athens home, where she has lived since 1945.

Della Huff's former house in East Athens, near Georgia Drive—Photo by Donny Bailey Seagraves

Despite a lack of material wealth and possessions, Miss Della says, "I always had a good time. Most all the neighbors used to come to Mama's house to visit. Back then, everybody was just as good as gold."

Not only were people better years ago, but according to Della, the food was much better as well. "My mother always kept three cows, so we had plenty of milk and butter. That white, puffy butter she turned was the best stuff! We don't have butter like that no more. Never will."

Della is hard of hearing now, and her skin has weathered and mellowed into shades of pink, tan, and white. But she still takes care of herself. And she still calls everyone darling.

Studying a picture of herself taken in the early 1900s when she was a teenager, Della laughs softly. "I thought I was all grown up in that picture. I wish I was like that now."[1]

Apple Upside Down Cake

- *1/2 cup margarine*
- *1 cup sugar*
- *2 eggs*
- *1 teaspoon vanilla*
- *2 cups flour (plain)*
- *1 teaspoon baking powder*
- *1 teaspoon soda*
- *1 cup sour cream (8 ounces)*
- *1 (7 ounce) jar marshmallow creme*
- *1 tablespoon lemon juice*
- *1 1/2 teaspoons cinnamon*
- *2 cups peeled apple slices*
- *1 cup chopped nuts*

Beat margarine and sugar until fluffy and light. Add eggs, one at a time, mixing well after each addition. Blend in vanilla. Add combined flour, baking powder, soda alternately with sour cream, mixing well after each addition. Combine marshmallow creme, lemon juice and cinnamon, mixing with electric mixer until well-blended. Layer half apples, nuts, marshmallow creme mixture and batter in well-greased ten-inch tube pan. Repeat with other half. Bake in 350-degree oven for one hour. Immediately loosen cake from rim of pan and put on serving plate.

Note: You can substitute a greased thirteen-inch by nine-inch by two-inch pan. Spread one-half batter on bottom of pan. Top with apples, nuts, marshmallow creme mixture and remaining batter. Bake at 350 degrees for forty-five minutes. Cool and cut into squares. —*Anne Seagraves, Clarke County, Georgia*

Front row, L-R: Sandy Seagraves, Suzanne Seagraves Gerling. Back row, L-R: Phillip Seagraves, Lori Fields Loden, Jimmy Fields, Mary Seagraves Fields, Jo Dobbins Seagraves—From Sandy Seagraves

Fresh Apple Cake

- *2 cups sugar*
- *1 1/2 cups Crisco oil*
- *3 eggs*
- *1 teaspoon salt*
- *2 teaspoons cinnamon*
- *3 cups (chopped) apples*
- *3 cups (sifted) plain flour*
- *1 cup (chopped) nuts*
- *1 teaspoon soda*
- *2 teaspoons vanilla*

Mix sugar, oil and eggs together with a fork. Then add dry ingredients. Fold in apples, nuts and vanilla. Bake in greased tube pan at 350 degrees for one hour.

Topping

- *1 cup brown sugar*
- *1/4 cup sweet milk*
- *1/2 cup margarine*

Mix in a saucepan. Boil over moderate heat for three minutes. Make holes in cake while hot and pour topping over cake.—*Anne Seagraves, Clarke County, Georgia*

Grandmama's Apple Cake

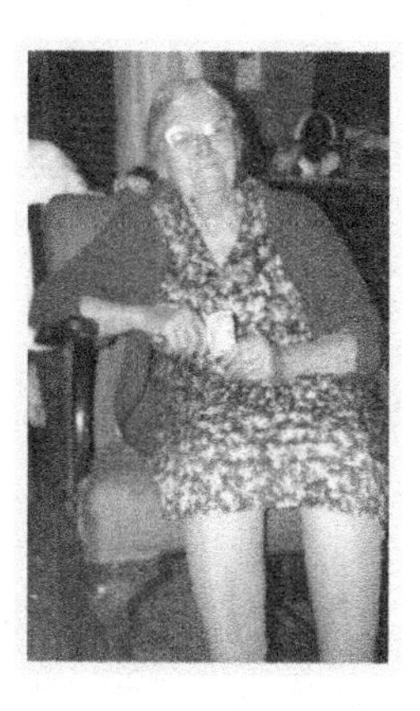

Ethel Strickland Pettyjohn —From Norris Family photo albums

- *2 sticks margarine*
- *2 cups sugar*
- *2 eggs*
- *2 cups all-purpose flour*
- *2 teaspoons (each) soda, cinnamon and vanilla*
- *4 teaspoons lemon juice*
- *4 cups (chopped and peeled) apple*

Combine first three ingredients and beat one minute. Mix dry ingredients and add to creamed mixture. Add remaining ingredients and mix well. Pour into greased and floured thirteen by nine by two-inch baking pan and bake in preheated 350-degree oven for one hour.—*Ethel Strickland Pettyjohn, Clarke County, Georgia*

Sitting on the Georgia Drive house porch. L-R: Nelson "Petie" Seagraves with his granddaughters Suzanne Seagraves Gerling and Sandy Seagraves—From Sandy Seagraves

Cake Recipe for Olden Days

- *4 cups (sifted) cake flour*
- *5 teaspoons baking powder*
- *1 1/2 teaspoons salt*
- *6 egg whites*
- *1/2 cup sugar*
- *1 1/2 cups milk or 2 cups*
- *1 cup shortening (Crisco) or butter*
- *2 cups sugar*
- *2 teaspoons vanilla*
- *With butter, use 1 1/2 cups milk. With shortening, use 2 cups milk.*

Measure sifted flour, add baking powder and salt and sift together three times. Beat egg whites until foamy. Add one-half-cup sugar gradually and cream until light and fluffy. Add flour mixture alternately with milk, a small amount at a time, until smooth. Add vanilla, then add egg whites and beat thoroughly into batter.

Pour into three nine-inch pans that have been lined with waxed paper. Bake in 375-degree oven twenty to twenty-five minutes. Cool layers and spread two layers with lemon filling and top layer with seven-minute frosting. (Note: This cake made with shortening isn't good.)

Grandchildren in Annie D's Georgia Drive kitchen, L-R: Greg Seagraves, Suzanne Seagraves Gerling, her husband Joe Gerling, Jen Seagraves, Travis Fields

Lemon Filling

- *3/4 cup sugar*
- *1/4 cup cornstarch*
- *1/4 teaspoon salt*
- *1 egg yolk (slightly beaten)*
- *1 cup water*
- *1/3 cup lemon juice (fresh)*
- *1 tablespoon butter*
- *1 teaspoon grated lemon rind*

Combine sugar, cornstarch and salt in top of double boiler. Blend egg yolks, water and lemon juice in small bowl. Add sugar mixture gradually, blending well. Cook over boiling water about five minutes or until mixture thickens, stirring constantly. Remove from heat and

add butter and lemon rind. Cool slightly before spreading on cake.
—*Anne Seagraves, Clarke County, Georgia*

Annie D enjoying a holiday meal with her twin grandchildren Jen and Greg Seagraves and their uncle Mike Bailey in the Seagraves' Winterville house

Seven Minute Frosting

- *2 egg whites (unbeaten)*
- *1 1/2 cups sugar*
- *Dash of salt*
- *1/3 cups water*
- *2 teaspoons white corn syrup*

Evalena Strickland Wynn and husband Edwin Wynn standing in the front yard of their East Athens, Georgia home at the corner of Poplar and Branch Streets. In the background, to the left, is what later came to be known as the R.E.M. Murmur Trestle. Evalena and Edwin were the parents of Reba Winn (sometimes spelled Wynn) Seagraves. Evalena was a sister of Mahulda "Hulda" Strickland Coile, Donny Bailey Seagraves' great-grandmother.—From Hope Seagraves Austin

Put salt, water and corn syrup in top of double boiler. Beat one minute until thoroughly mixed. Then place over boiling water and beat constantly with electric beater for seven minutes or until done. —*Anne Seagraves, Clarke County, Georgia*

Chocolate Cake

- *2 cups sugar*

- *1 cup Crisco*
- *4 eggs*
- *3 cups sifted (White Lily) plain flour*
- *3 teaspoons baking powder*
- *1 cup sweet milk*
- *1 teaspoon vanilla*
- *1 teaspoon lemon*
- *1/4 teaspoon salt*

Cream sugar with Crisco. Add eggs, one at a time. Beat and add flavoring, then add flour that has baking powder and salt added to it. Add milk and beat real good. Put into four pans (eight or nine inches).

Chocolate Icing

- *2 cups sugar*
- *1/4 cup cocoa*
- *1/2 cup Crisco*
- *2/3 cup can cream*

Add (one teaspoon vanilla after it cooks). Mix and bring to a boil and cook two minutes. Stir all the time while it's cooking.—*Anne Seagraves, Clarke County, Georgia*

Dump Cake

- *1-pint fruit (your choice)*
- *1 large box Jello (your choice)*
- *1 box cake mix (yellow or white)*
- *1 cup water*
- *1 stick margarine*

Mix and dump into thirteen by nine by 2-inch pan and bake until toothpick comes out clean.—*Anne Seagraves, Clarke County, Georgia*

Taylor Loden and her twin brother Austin Loden—From Taylor Loden

Fruit Cocktail Cake

- *1 box yellow cake mix*
- *2 1/2 cups coconut*
- *1 (16-ounce) can of fruit cocktail*
- *2 eggs*
- *1/2 cup firmly packed brown sugar*
- *1/2 cup butter*
- *1/2 cup sugar*
- *1/2 cup evaporated milk*

Combine cake mix, fruit cocktail with syrup, one cup coconut, and the eggs in large mixing bowl. Blend, then beat at medium speed for 2 minutes. Pour into greased nine by thirteen by two-inch pan and bake at 325 degrees for forty-five minutes.

Topping

Bring butter, one-half cup sugar and milk to a boil in a small saucepan. Boil two minutes. Remove from heat and stir in the remaining coconut. Spoon over hot cake in pan. Serve warm or cold. —*Anne Seagraves, Clarke County, Georgia*

Lucille Huff's Cake Recipe

- *2 cups sugar*
- *1 cup Crisco*
- *4 eggs*
- *1/4 teaspoon salt*
- *2 1/2 teaspoons baking powder*
- *3 cups plain flour (sifted White Lily)*
- *1 cup sweet milk (a little canned milk added)*
- *1 teaspoon lemon flavoring*
- *1 teaspoon vanilla*

Cream Crisco and sugar together. Add eggs, one at a time, beating well after each addition. Add flour, which has the baking powder added, and also the salt. Add milk and beat real good. Bake in three or four eight-inch pans at 350 degrees until straw comes out clean.

Frosting

- *2 cups sugar*
- *1 small can canned milk*
- *1/2 cup Crisco*
- *1/4 cocoa*

Mix sugar and cocoa. Add Crisco and cream. Mix all ingredients except vanilla, and bring to a boil. Boil exactly two minutes. Stir all the time while cooking. Add vanilla after cooking.—*Lucille Huff, Clarke County, Georgia*

Climax Hosiery Mill

An undated aerial photo of the former Climax Hosiery Mill building (later Stitchcraft Sewing Plant). The mill building is the large brick structure near the bottom, center right, next to the Oconee River. Also visible to the left, near the bottom, is St. Mary's Episcopal Church, location of the first R.E.M. band's concert. This photo was commissioned by and once owned by Robert "Bob" Schindel, former owner of Stitchcraft.—From Phillip Seagraves

By the time you read this, the old Climax Hosiery Mill building will be gone. The sprawling red brick structure which stood by the muddy Oconee River for so many years will be a useless pile of broken bricks and ancient timbers discarded, tossed away like common debris. And the spot of earth where the mill used to stand will be raw, red dirt, musty-smelling, and exposed to the sun and human eyes for the first time in decades.

Here is the first half of a panoramic photo of Climax Hosiery Mill employees in front of the mill building. It was taken circa 1940s. First woman on the left, third row, is Willie Belle Pettyjohn Strickland, Annie D's sister.

Yes, the old Climax Hosiery Mill no longer exists, except in the memories of hundreds of local people, men and women who spent many of their best years working there.

William Ephraim Pettyjohn, my husband's maternal grandfather, came down from the mountains of Dalton, Georgia, to work, first at Rogers Hosiery Mill, then at the Climax Hosiery Mill, after the Dalton mill closed, putting him out of work. A neat, stern-looking man, he was a "fixer" (mechanic), someone who kept the looper machines going.

My husband's other grandfather, Harvey Lee "Bob" Seagraves, also worked at the mill, beginning as a floor sweeper and working his way up to superintendent, in charge of the entire mill. His son, Nelson "Petie" Seagraves, my husband's father, worked for over thirty years in the dye room at the mill, mixing chemicals and dyes for socks. He met his wife, Anne "Annie D" Pettyjohn, there. It was common for entire families to work at the mill back then.

Here is the second half of the Climax Hosiery Mill panoramic photo. Bottom row, second from right, Nelson "Petie" Seagraves. Third row, near the center is Leonard "Tensie" Seagraves and Frank Ed Seagraves. Back row, first on the right, Harvey Hill "Sleepy" Seagraves. Back row, first on the left, Harvey Lee "Bob" Seagraves. There are many other Seagraves, Hansfords, Wynns, Stricklands and neighbors and friends of Annie D and Petie Seagraves' in these two Climax Hosiery Mill photos.

"Many people think my daddy, Alonzo Dudley, started the Climax Hosiery Mill," Gordon Dudley told me the other day. "But he didn't. A Mr. English started it. The mill used to be in the building where Tony's Restaurant was downtown. Then it moved down here.

"This," he said, gesturing toward the part of the mill building closest to the river bridge, "used to be two stories high. They tore off the top story and modified it when they moved the mill here. Daddy became the owner after Mr. English left."

A few years after Mr. Dudley's father died, the mill closed.

Mr. Robert "Bob" Schindel came down from New York originally to work at a mill in Dalton, Georgia. Before the Climax Hosiery Mill closed, he ran a small sewing operation in the basement.

"I bought the building in 1969," Bob said. "And we moved upstairs when the mill closed. We were here for twenty-six years."

This antique yarn spinner on top of the Pettyjohn Hoosier kitchen cabinet was given to Phillip Seagraves by Gordon Dudley not long before the Climax Hosiery/Stitchcraft building was demolished to make way for an apartment complex. Mr. Dudley said it was the oldest piece of memorabilia still left in the building and might have come from the previous mill there.—Photo by Donny Bailey Seagraves

Many local people worked at Bob and Reba Schindel's sewing plant, Stitchcraft, over the years, including me, as a payroll clerk for about six months in the 1970s. Walking for the last time across the narrow wooden floorboards worn slick with the footsteps of my husband's family and all the other local people who worked at Climax Hosiery Mill and Stitchcraft over the years, I could almost smell the sweat of hard work in the air. I could almost hear the sharp racket of the knitting machines and the whirling sounds of sewing machines filling the old building with life again.

By the time you read this, the windows will be gone and there will be nothing left to hold back the sky. The old mill's time has passed. It exists no more except in the memories of people who made it a part of their lives. They will carry it with them always.[2]

Harvey Lee "Bob" Seagraves and his second wife Reba Winn Seagraves. Bob was a longtime superintendent at Climax Hosiery Mill.—From Hope Seagraves Austin

Georgia Pecan Cake

- *2 cups butter*
- *4 eggs (separated)*
- *4 1/2 cups (sifted) plain flour*
- *1/4 teaspoon salt*
- *1/2 cup milk*
- *1 pound box brown sugar*
- *1 teaspoon vanilla*
- *3 tablespoons instant coffee*
- *3 tablespoons hot water*
- *4 cups (chopped) pecans*
- *1 teaspoon baking powder*

Soften butter at room temperature. Sift flour, salt and baking powder together. Separate eggs and beat yolks until they are lemony colored. Beat whites until they form stiff peaks. In large mixing bowl, cream butter and brown sugar. Add egg yolks, mixing well. Dissolve instant coffee in hot water and then mix with milk and vanilla. Add alternately with dry ingredients. Mix well after each addition. Fold in egg whites and pecans. Bake in oiled and floured ten-inch tube pan for one hour and thirty minutes at 325 degrees.—*Anne Seagraves, Clarke County, Georgia*

Athletic Seagraves

A long ago Athens High School football team photo taken when the school was on Prince Avenue. On the front row, first left, is Harold Seagraves.—From Freddy Seagraves

Many Seagraves descendants have excelled at athletics, including Nelson "Petie" Seagraves, Frank Ed Seagraves and Harold Seagraves, who were all outstanding baseball players in their younger years. Harold also played football at Athens High School, as did David

Seagraves and Donald Seagraves. Their sister, Barbara Seagraves Tiller Carter, played basketball at Athens High School. Judd Farr and Richard DeRose, among others, excelled at football, baseball, basketball and/or track. Suzanne Seagraves Gerling, Carla Wade, Lori Fields Loden and Gena Farr Haskell are all excellent equestrians.

Athens Album

Winning Team

This photo of the Climax Hosiery Mill fast-pitch softball city championship team was made in 1946 at the Lyndon House on Hoyt Street, where the championship game was played. Pictured (front row, L-R) are: Ed Hansford, Ucalee Cape, Dupree Wilkes, Coy Lee Jordon, and Charlie Owens. Back row (L-R): Clarence Cornelison, Richard Saye, "Dee" Allen, "Tensie" Seagraves, Petie Seagraves, "Red" Warwick, and Manager Joe Saye. In the July 13 Classic Scene, we ran a photo of part of the Home Economics Department at Athens High School. At the time, we were unable to identify the students in the photo. We have been informed that they are Marlene Kicklighter, Emily Sims, and Sarah Wilkins.

The Climax Hosiery Mill fast-pitch softball City of Athens championship team in 1946. On the front row, left side, is Ed Hansford. Next to him is Ucalee Cape. In the back row, fourth left, is Tensie Seagraves and next to him is Nelson "Petie" Seagraves.

The Climax Hosiery Mill fast-pitch softball team won the City of Athens championship in 1946. Several Seagraves family members played on that legendary team, including Ed Hansford, a son of Lula Seagraves Hansford and father of Jimmy, Billy and Susan, and Tensie Seagraves, father of Brenda Seagraves.

The 1950 Athens City Champions pose in front of Oconee Street Elementary School. Front row, L-R: unidentified, unidentified, unidentified, Nelson "Petie" Seagraves, Bill Giles, unidentified, Wallace Seagraves, Frank Ed Seagraves. Back row, L-R: Coach Joe Saye, Len Seagraves, Wheeler Hawkins, Danny Farr, James Hansford, unidentified, Woodie Gann, Ralph Hill, Coach Eldridge Smith. (Note: Some of the identification here is from the book, Across The River: The People, Places and Culture of East Athens *by Maxine Pinson Easom and Patsy Hawkins Arnold)*

Nelson "Petie" Seagraves, dad to Billy, Mary and Phillip, played on this team as well. Another member of the team, Ucalee Cape, many years later became the second husband of Anne D Seagraves' younger sister Mary Pettyjohn Norris Cape.

This group picture includes several Seagraves family members who excelled at sports. Front row, L-R: Unknown, Billy Seagraves, David Seagraves. Back row, L-R: Frank Ed Seagraves, Donald Seagraves.

Goofy Cake

First Layer

Mix and press into greased nine by thirteen by two-inch baking pan:

- *1 box yellow cake mix*
- *1 stick margarine or butter*
- *2 eggs (beaten)*

Second Layer

Sprinkle over first layer in pan:

- *1 cup (chopped) pecans*

- *1 cup coconut*
- *1 cup chocolate chips*

Third Layer

Mix the following and spread on second layer:

- *1 box powdered sugar (sifted)*
- *1 eight-ounce package cream cheese (softened)*
- *2 eggs (beaten)*

Bake at 350 degrees thirty-five or forty-five minutes. Cool and cut into squares. Serves fifteen to twenty people. It's very rich!—*Anne Seagraves, Clarke County, Georgia*

Three generations at a long ago Christmas party at the Seagraves' house on Georgia Drive. Anne "Annie D" Seagraves is in the middle with her daughter Mary Seagraves Fields to her left and her granddaughter Lori Fields Loden to her right.—Photo by Donny Bailey Seagraves

The Impossible Cake

- *4 eggs*
- *1 cup shredded coconut*
- *1/2 cup sugar*
- *1/2 stick (melted) margarine*
- *1/2 cup baking mix*
- *2 cups milk*
- *1 teaspoon vanilla*

Mix all ingredients in blender and blend at low speed for thirty seconds. Pour into ungreased pie plate. Bake at 350 degrees for fifty minutes.—*Anne Seagraves, Clarke County, Georgia*

> "I remember during the Christmas holidays, my mom Annie D and I going over to Aunt Clela Seagraves' house on Peter Street and making lots of cakes in that big kitchen. Mom loved to cook desserts and carried on the cake-making tradition at our Georgia Drive house after Aunt Clela died. Each Christmas, she spent days making at least four or five different cakes. Some of her favorites were coconut cake, orange slice cake, Milky Way cake and pound cake."
>
> — Mary Seagraves Fields

Japanese Fruitcake

- *1 cup butter or 2 sticks margarine*
- *2 cups sugar*
- *1/2 teaspoon salt*
- *4 eggs*

- *1 teaspoon cinnamon*
- *1 cup buttermilk*
- *1 teaspoon allspice*
- *3 cups flour*
- *1 teaspoon cloves*
- *1 cup (chopped) raisins*
- *1 teaspoon nutmeg*
- *1 cup (chopped) nuts*
- *1 teaspoon soda*

Cream butter and sugar together. Add eggs, one at a time, beating well after each addition. Sift dry ingredients together and add alternately with buttermilk. Add to creamed mixture. With one-fourth cup additional flour, dust raisins and nuts and add to mixture. Pour into three greased and floured layer cake pans. Bake at 300 degrees about one hour or until cake leaves side of pan. Cool on racks.

Filling

- *2 1/2 cups sugar*
- *2 tablespoons flour*
- *2 lemons (grated rind and juice)*
- *1 1/2 cups hot water*
- *2 cups coconut*

Combine all ingredients and cook until thick. Cool slightly, then spread between layers of cake.—*Anne Seagraves, Clarke County, Georgia*

Milky Way Cake

- *1/2 pound margarine (2 sticks)*
- *2 cups sugar*

- *4 eggs*
- *1/2 teaspoon soda mixed with 1 1/4 cups buttermilk*
- *2 1/2 cups plain flour*
- *1 cup (chopped) nuts*
- *4 Milky Way candy bars*

Melt candy in one stick margarine. Cream sugar and one stick margarine. Add eggs one at a time. Add flour and buttermilk mixture. Add melted candy with mixture, and then add nuts. Bake in three or four nine-inch pans that have been floured and greased. Bake in 325-degree oven for thirty or forty minutes or until done.

Annie D's daughter-in-law Jo Seagraves with Mary Seagraves Fields, Annie D's daughter, in the Georgia Drive house kitchen

Frosting

- *2 1/2 cups sugar*
- *1 cup evaporated milk*
- *1 stick margarine*
- *6 ounces chocolate chips*

- *1 cup marshmallow creme*

Mix over low heat. Combine sugar and milk and cook until soft ball state. Add chips and marshmallow creme and stir until chips melt. Remove from heat and beat until cool. Frost and stack.—*Anne Seagraves, Clarke County, Georgia*

Annie D opening presents during a long ago Georgia Drive house Christmas party. In the background, is her grandson Kevin Fields, talking on the phone and waving.—Photo by Donny Bailey Seagraves

Orange Slice Cake

- *1 cup margarine*
- *2 cups sugar*
- *4 eggs*
- *1 teaspoon soda in 1/2 cup buttermilk*
- *3 1/2 cups plain flour*
- *1 pound dates (chopped)*
- *1 pound candy orange slices (chopped)*
- *2 cups nuts (chopped)*
- *1 cup coconut*

Annie D in her Winterville kitchen with her children. L-R: Phillip Seagraves, Mary Seagraves Fields, Annie D, Billy Seagraves

Cream margarine and sugar until smooth. Add eggs one at a time and beat well after each addition. Add buttermilk to creamed mixture. Place flour in large bowl. Add dates, orange slices, nuts and coconut. Stir to coat each piece. Add flour to creamed mixture. This makes a very stiff dough that should be mixed with your hands. Put in a greased and floured tube cake pan. Bake at 250 degrees for two and one-half to three hours. Leave cake in pan until cool.

Topping

Combine one cup of fresh orange juice and two cups of powdered sugar. Punch holes in cake and pour over cake while still hot.—*Anne Seagraves, Clarke County, Georgia*

Annie D's favorite pound cake

"Mom used to make her favorite pound cake a lot, and we all loved it. But sometimes, it would flop and she'd open the door and throw that cake out in the backyard for the birds to eat. Then she'd go back in the kitchen and make another one."

— Billy Seagraves

Anne's Favorite Pound Cake

- *1 cup Crisco*
- *1/2 pound butter or 2 sticks margarine*
- *3 cups sugar*
- *Pinch of salt*
- *5 eggs*
- *1 cup sweet milk*
- *3 cups plain flour with 1 teaspoon baking powder*
- *1 teaspoon butternut flavoring*

Cream Crisco and margarine. Add sugar. Add eggs one at a time. Add flour, milk and flavoring. Bake one hour and twenty-five minutes in greased tube pan at 325 degrees.

Frosting (Optional — this cake tastes great without it.)

- *3/4 stick margarine*
- *4 tablespoons canned milk*
- *1 box (sifted) powdered sugar*
- *1 cup (grated) nuts*

Mix well and spread all over cake, including top and sides. —*Anne Seagraves, Clarke County, Georgia*

Billy Seagraves and his younger brother Phillip Seagraves

Blueberry Pound Cake

- *8-ounce cream cheese softened*
- *1/2 cup vegetable oil*
- *18-ounce package yellow butter cake mix*
- *3-ounce package instant vanilla pudding mix*

- *4 eggs, beaten*
- *2 teaspoons vanilla flavoring*
- *2 cups fresh or frozen blueberries, thawed*

Preheat oven to 325 degrees. Lightly spray a nine-inch tube pan or Bundt pan and dust with flour. Combine cream cheese and oil. Beat with mixer on high speed until smooth and creamy. Add cake mix, pudding mix, eggs and vanilla flavoring. Beat at medium speed until blended. Fold in berries. Batter will be very thick. Spoon into pan. Bake sixty minutes. Check with toothpick. Cool.—*Ann Seagraves, Madison County, Georgia*

Ann Shellnut Seagraves with her sister Eleanor—From Tristin Seagraves Johnson

Chocolate Chip or Butterscotch Chip Pound Cake

- *18-ounce package of yellow cake mix*
- *3-ounce package of instant chocolate pudding mix or butterscotch pudding mix*
- *8-ounce carton sour cream*
- *3 eggs beaten*
- *3/4 cup vegetable oil*
- *3/4 cup water*

- *1 teaspoon vanilla extract*
- *6 ounces milk chocolate chips*

Travis Fields, youngest son of Mary Seagraves Fields and Jimmy Fields, with his wife Tara Gabriel Fields and their daughters Ally Fields and Laney Fields

In a large mixing bowl, combine cake mix, pudding mix, sour cream, eggs, oil, water and vanilla. Beat until well-blended. Fold in chocolate chips or butterscotch chips. Spray baking pan or dish with Bakers Joy and then pour batter into the pan. Bake at 350 degrees for forty to forty-five minutes. Remove cake and allow to cool.—*Ann Seagraves, Madison County, Georgia*

Pound Cake

- *3 cups cake flour*
- *3 cups sugar*
- *5 large eggs*
- *1 1/4 cups Crisco*

- *1 cup sweet milk*
- *1 teaspoon baking powder*
- *1 teaspoon vanilla*

Nash Austin, son of Wayne and Hope Seagraves Austin, with wife Shelley Majors Austin and their children Majors Winn Austin and Lucas Day Austin—From Hope Seagraves Austin

Cream sugar and Crisco. Add eggs, one at a time, creaming well after each addition. Alternate flour and milk and add vanilla. Bake one hour and fifteen minutes in flour and greased tube pan at 325 degrees.—*Melissa Hawkins Seagraves, Madison County, Georgia*

Pecan Pound Cake

- *1 box butter pecan cake mix*
- *2 cans coconut pecan cake frosting*
- *3/4 cup vegetable oil*
- *4 eggs*
- *1 cup water*

Preheat oven to 350 degrees. Mix all ingredients with electric mixer. Grease tube pan and dust with one-fourth cup confectioners' sugar.

Pour batter into pan and bake (using recommended time on cake mix box) at 350 degrees, then check with a toothpick to see when it's done. Cool at least ten minutes, then frost with second can of coconut pecan cake frosting.—*Ann Seagraves, Madison County, Georgia*

Banana Pudding Cake

- *1 box yellow cake mix: (Bake the cake following the directions on the box.)*
- *2 (3/4 ounce) packages instant banana pudding mix*
- *4 cups milk*
- *1 (8-ounce) carton of Cool Whip*
- *30 vanilla wafers (crushed)*

Cousins Carla Wade and Jen Seagraves—From Jen Seagraves

Prepare cake according to directions, using a nine by thirteen-inch cake pan. Once cake is out of oven, allow it to cool for five minutes. Using a wooden spoon handle, poke holes in the cake. Be sure the holes are large and deep enough to allow the pudding to get down through the cake to the bottom of the pan.

In a bowl, whisk together four cups of milk with the Cool Whip and with the banana pudding mix. Make sure all the lumps are gone. When the pudding just begins to thicken, pour pudding over the cake. Make sure the pudding goes down through all the holes in the cake.

When the cake is cool, spread whipped topping over it. Crush the vanilla wafers and sprinkle over the Cool Whip topping. Ready to serve.—*Ann Seagraves, Madison County, Georgia*

Nelson "Petie" Seagraves with his grandchildren in the Georgia Drive house living room. Bottom row, L-R: Kevin Fields, Suzanne Seagraves Gerling. Second row, L-R: Travis Fields, Nelson "Petie" Seagraves, Sandy Seagraves, Lori Fields Loden. Not pictured: Petie and Annie D's youngest grandchildren, fraternal twins Jen and Greg Seagraves.

Creole Chocolate Cake

- *2 cups unsifted all-purpose flour*
- *1 teaspoon soda*
- *1/2 cup butter or margarine*
- *1/2 cup salad oil*
- *3 squares unsweetened chocolate*
- *2 cups sugar*
- *1/2 cup sour milk*
- *2 eggs (beaten)*
- *1 teaspoon vanilla*

- Place one and one-half teaspoons vinegar in a one-cup measuring cup and fill with milk to measure one-half cup.

Preheat oven to 350 degrees. Sift flour with soda into large bowl. Grease well and flour two eight by eight by two-inch square pans. In small saucepan, combine butter, oil and chocolate. Stir over low heat to melt the chocolate. Add one cup water. Cool fifteen minutes.

To flour mixture, add two cups sugar, the eggs, sour milk and one teaspoon vanilla. Mix with wooden spoon. Stir in cooled chocolate just to combine. Quickly turn into prepared pans. Bake thirty to thirty-five minutes till surface springs back when pressed with finger. Cool in pans five minutes.

Filling

- *1 small can evaporated milk*
- *3/4 cup sugar*
- *1/4 cup chopped raisins*
- *1/2 cup chopped dates*
- *1 teaspoon vanilla*
- *1/2 cup chopped walnut or pecans*
- *1/2 cup chilled heavy cream*

Frosting

- *1 package 6 ounces semisweet chocolate chips*
- *1/2 cup sour cream*
- *Dash of salt*

In a small saucepan, combine milk, sugar and one-fourth cup water. Cook over medium heat, stirring to dissolve sugar. Add raisins and dates. Stir with wooden spoon. Cook stirring until mixture thickens, about five minutes. Add vanilla and nuts. Cool completely.

In small bowl, beat cream just until stiff. On plate, place layer top-side down. Spread with filling, then whipped cream. Top with second layer. To make frosting, melt chocolate in top of double boiler over hot water. Remove top of boiler. Stir in sour cream and salt. With wooden spoon, beat until smooth. Cool five minutes. Spread on cakes. Refrigerate one hour before serving.—*Anne Seagraves, Clarke County, Georgia*

Sweet Potato Surprise Cake

- *1 cup vegetable oil*
- *2 cups sugar*
- *4 eggs (separated)*
- *1/4 cup hot water*
- *2 1/2 cups (sifted) cake flour*
- *1 tablespoon baking powder*
- *1/4 teaspoon salt*
- *1 teaspoon cinnamon*
- *1 teaspoon nutmeg*
- *1 1/2 cups grated raw sweet potatoes*
- *1 cup chopped walnuts or pecans*
- *1 teaspoon vanilla*

Combine oil, sugar, egg yolks and water and beat at medium speed until mixed well. Combine dry ingredients and add to oil mixture. Mix just until moistened. Stir in sweet potatoes, nuts and vanilla. Beat egg whites until stiff but not dry. Fold into batter. Spoon batter into three greased nine-inch cake pans and bake at 350 degrees for twenty-five to thirty minutes.

~

Lori Fields Loden's Memories

Seagraves family members gathered around the table in the Georgia Drive house kitchen. L-R, clockwise: Lori Fields Loden, her mother Mary Seagraves Fields, her brother Travis Fields, her uncle Billy Seagraves and his daughter Suzanne Seagraves Gerling. Lori is the daughter of Jimmy and Mary Seagraves Fields, granddaughter of Nelson "Petie" and Annie D Seagraves and great-granddaughter of Harvey Lee "Bob" and Julia Suddeth Seagraves.—Photo by Donny Bailey Seagraves

215 Georgia Drive
Garden Spot of the World

Food

- Thanksgiving gathering and meal
- Christmas gathering and meal
- All the delicious food and desserts
- Grandmother's famous sweet tea

- Double-decker fudge
- Divinity candy
- Coconut cake
- Homemade biscuits
- Country ham
- Red-eye gravy
- Chicken Mull (a favorite of everyone!)
- BBQ goat meat (Grandad's favorite)
- Granddad's perfectly grilled steak dinner, which consisted of three things: T-Bone steak, "marble slab thick," sesame seed BBQ bread, and Grandmother's seven-ingredient salad (lettuce, cucumber, onion, garlic, cheese, bell pepper and tomato, tossed with Four Seasons Italian dressing).

Lori Fields Loden in her grandmother's Georgia Drive kitchen

Memories

- Thanksgiving and Christmas with family
- Friends and family visiting
- Snoopy, their dachshund puppy dog

- Playing card games at the round antique oak kitchen table
- Antique store furniture hunting
- Weekends at their house, waking up to breakfast cooking with country music playing on the radio.
- Fishing at their friends' local lakes and petting horses at one lake!
- Sitting in the big metal front porch swing and listening to the Georgia Bulldog football game that was being played live over the hill in nearby Sanford Stadium!
- Walking through Oconee Hill Cemetery with Grandmother and Granddad, visiting family graves
- Picking roses from the rosebushes along their fenced-in backyard
- All of us grandchildren exploring the attic
- Visiting Granddad at Clarke County Milling Company (where he worked later on during retirement) and always going straight to the horse tack room
- Their 50th wedding anniversary celebration at Oconee Street Methodist Church
- 1976 Daytona trip with Grandmother and Granddad
- Driving on Daytona Beach
- Visiting their friends and eating fresh shrimp and seafood
- Shopping at Daytona flea markets
- Visiting the Daytona Speedway

Grandmother Anne's Favorite Things

- The Atlanta Braves
- Pearls
- "Clip-on" earrings
- Chanel No. 5 perfume
- Giorgio Beverly Hills perfume
- Revlon "Cherries in the Snow" lipstick

- Queen Anne chocolate-covered cherries
- Dr. Pepper soft drink

Granddad Petie's Favorite Things

- The Georgia Bulldogs
- His silver and red "Georgia Bulldogs" truck
- Gin and rummy card games
- *Wheel of Fortune* gameshow (he would always call it the spin game)
- Vienna sausages and potted meat with crackers

Granddad Petie's Favorite Sayings

- "Ringy Dingy Do" song and dance
- "Sambo and Kitty" song
- "Good food, good meat, good gosh, let's eat! Get on with it!"—Lori Fields Seagraves

Lori Fields Loden enjoying a day at a pumpkin patch with daughter Taylor.—From Lori Fields Loden

Jo Dobbins Seagraves looks on as husband Billy takes a bite of his mother Annie D's coconut cake.

Coconut Cake

- *1 box Duncan Hines Butter cake mix*
- *2 cups sugar*
- *2 cups sour cream*
- *2 (9-ounce) bags frozen coconut*
- *1 1/2 cups Cool Whip (thawed)*

Bake cake as directed. Split layers in half. Combine sugar, sour cream and coconut (chill). Reserve one cup sour cream for frosting. Spread remaining between layers. Combine sour cream with Cool Whip. Blend until smooth. Put on top and sides. Store in airtight container and put in refrigerator for two or three days before serving.`

Creamy Coconut Frosting

- *1 (13-ounce) can evaporated milk*
- *1 cup sugar*
- *1/2 cup butter or margarine*

- *3 egg yolks*
- *1 teaspoon vanilla*
- *1 1/2 cups coconut*

Combine milk, sugar, butter, egg yolks and vanilla in heavy saucepan. Cook over medium heat for two minutes. Remove from heat and stir in coconut. Frost cake.—*Anne Seagraves, Clarke County, Georgia*

Another Version of Coconut Filling

- *3 whole eggs*
- *1 1/2 cups sugar*
- *1 cup milk*
- *2 1/2 cups coconut (fresh or frozen)*
- *1 teaspoon vanilla*

Beat eggs. Add sugar, milk and coconut. Stir and cook to custard consistency. Add vanilla. Cool and spread between cake layers and on top of cake. Sprinkle with additional coconut.—*Anne Seagraves, Clarke County, Georgia*

Coconut Cake Supreme

- *1 box white Pillsbury cake mix with pudding*
- *1 can sweetened condensed milk (Eagle Brand)*
- *1 can cream of coconut*
- *1 (9-ounce) carton Cool Whip*
- *Coconut*

Make cake according to instructions on box. Immediately after removing cake from the oven, make numerous holes all over the cake (all the way to the bottom). While hot, pour condensed milk and cream of coconut in holes. Allow it to cool. Spread Cool Whip over top. Add coconut. Must be refrigerated.—*Anne Seagraves, Clarke County, Georgia*

Lucille Gann, Annie D's longtime next-door neighbor, was a favorite visitor at the Georgia Drive house.

Sunshine Spice Cake

- *1 cup brown sugar*
- *1 cup sour milk*
- *1/2 teaspoon soda*
- *2 eggs, reserving one yolk for frosting*
- *2 teaspoons each of cinnamon and baking powder*
- *1 teaspoon of cloves*
- *1/2 teaspoon nutmeg*
- *1 and 7/8 cups flour*

Mix in the order given and bake in layers.

Frosting for Sunshine Cake

Mix one and one-third cups confectioner's sugar, one teaspoon melted butter, one egg yolk and enough thin cream to make the consistency to spread. Place between layers and on top.—*Ethel Strickland Pettyjohn, Clarke County, Georgia*

Children's Cupcakes

- *1 cup self-rising flour*
- *1 cup ice cream (any flavor)*

Mix well and pour into muffin tins. Bake at 350 degrees until lightly browned.—*Anne Seagraves, Clarke County, Georgia*

Carrot Cake

- *2 cups plain flour*
- *2 teaspoons baking powder*
- *1 teaspoon salt*
- *2 teaspoons cinnamon*
- *1/2 teaspoon nutmeg*
- *Pinch of ground cloves*
- *4 eggs*
- *1 cup sugar*
- *3/4 cup firmly packed brown sugar*
- *1 teaspoon vanilla*
- *1 cup salad oil*
- *3 cups (1 pound) grated carrots*
- *3/4 cups (chopped) nuts - walnuts or pecans*

Preheat oven to 350 degrees. Grease and flour two (eight-inch) cake pans. In small bowl, combine flour, soda, salt, cinnamon, nutmeg and cloves. In large bowl, combine eggs, sugar and vanilla. Beat until smooth. With mixer at low speed, add oil in steady stream. Add flour mixture and beat until blended well. With spatula, fold in nuts and carrots. Spoon into pans and bake forty to forty-five minutes.

Cream Cheese Frosting

- *1 package (8 ounces) cream cheese, softened*
- *1/4 cup butter or margarine*
- *1 teaspoon vanilla*
- *1/2 cup grated orange peel*
- *3 cups powdered sugar*

In a large bowl, combine cream cheese, butter, vanilla and orange peel. Beat until light and smooth. Beat in powdered sugar to right consistency and spread on layers.—*Anne Seagraves, Clarke County, Georgia*

Caramel Cake Icing

- 1 cup buttermilk
- 2 cups sugar
- 1/2 teaspoon soda
- 1/2 cup butter
- 2 1/2 cups brown sugar
- 1 tablespoon vanilla

Mix sugars, butter and milk. Cook until it forms a soft ball. Cool. Add vanilla and beat until creamy. Don't beat it too long or let it get too thick. Frost yellow or white cake layers, whichever you prefer.—*Anne Seagraves, Clarke County, Georgia*

Harold Frederick "Freddy" Seagraves

Freddy Seagraves (in front) with his dad Harold Seagraves and older brother Bobby Seagraves—From Freddy Seagraves

Freddy Seagraves, youngest son of Harold and Mary Fred Warwick Seagraves, grandson of Harvey Lee "Bob" Seagraves and Julia Suddeth Seagraves and great-grandson of Hardy and Pink Carithers Seagraves, is well known in the Athens, Georgia music scene as drummer for the popular Jesters, a white soul/R&B band that lasted 50 years.

The Jesters formed in 1964, and among the bands and artists they either toured with or opened for were Jerry Butler, Marvin Gaye, Patti Labelle, The Marvelettes, The Platters and Jackie Wilson.

The Jesters band, front row, L-R: Freddy Seagraves, Bill Young. Middle row, L-R: Davis Causey, Donny Whitehead. Back row, L-R: Scott R. Piotrowski, Harold Williams, Bill McDonald, Cleon Nalley—From Freddy Seagraves

~

Cornbread Squares Cake

- *1 and 1/2 cups self-rising flour, sifted*
- *1 cup brown sugar, packed down*
- *1 cup vegetable oil*
- *4 eggs, well-beaten*
- *1 teaspoon vanilla extract*
- *1 cup chopped pecans*

Preheat oven to 350 degrees. Grease and flour (spray with Baker's Joy) a nine-by-thirteen-inch baking dish or pan. Set aside. In a mixing bowl, combine flour, sugar, oil, eggs, vanilla and chopped pecans. Mix well and pour into baking dish and spread evenly. Bake about thirty-five minutes or until done.—*Ann Seagraves, Madison County, Georgia*

Harold Seagraves with his three youngest children: Freddy Seagraves, Lynn Seagraves and Lisa Seagraves Layne—From Freddy Seagraves

Candied Fruitcake

- *3 packages (8 ounces each) pitted dates*
- *1 pound candied cherries*
- *1 pound candied pineapple*
- *8 cups (2 pounds) shelled pecan halves*
- *2 cups sifted flour (plain)*

- *3 teaspoons baking powder*
- *1/2 teaspoon salt*
- *4 eggs*
- *1 cup sugar*

Cut dates, cherries, pineapple and pecans into large pieces. Sift together flour, baking powder and salt. Beat eggs and gradually add sugar and flour mixture. Combine with fruit. Pack into pan that has been greased and lined with greased paper. Bake at 275 degrees for one hour and fifteen minutes. Makes five pounds. Use a big tube pan. —*Anne Seagraves, Clarke County, Georgia*

7 Up Cake

Mary Fred Warwick Seagraves, wife of Harold Seagraves and mother of Bobby, Freddy, Lynn and Lisa—From Freddy Seagraves

- *1 box lemon supreme cake mix*
- *1 box orange pineapple Jello*
- *4 eggs*
- *3/4 cup Crisco oil*
- *1 (10-ounce) bottle 7 Up*
- *1 small can crushed pineapple*
- *2 eggs*
- *1 stick butter*
- *1 1/4 cup sugar*
- *4 tablespoons flour*
- *1 can coconut or 1 (6-ounce) bag frozen coconut, thawed*

Mix well and bake the first five ingredients in a large long pan for forty minutes at 350 degrees. Cool. Then it's ready for the icing. To make the icing, heat last six ingredients. Cook slowly until thick and spread on cake. —*Anne Seagraves, Clarke County, Georgia*

German Chocolate Frosting

- *1 1/2 cans evaporated milk*
- *1 1/2 cups sugar*
- *4 slightly beaten egg yolks*
- *3/4 cup butter*
- *1 1/2 teaspoon vanilla*

Cook over medium heat, then add two cups coconut and one cup of nuts.—*Anne Seagraves, Clarke County, Georgia*

Sheet Cake Fillings and Icing

- *1 cup sugar or a little more*
- *1 stick butter*
- *1/2 cup canned cream*
- *1/2 cup coconut*
- *1/2 cup (chopped) nuts*

Mix all together and cook until soft ball stage. Drizzle over cake. —*Anne Seagraves, Clarke County, Georgia*

Coconut Filling for 3 Layer Cake

- *1/2 cup sugar*
- *1/4 teaspoon salt*
- *4 tablespoons flour*
- *1 cup milk*
- *1 small can evaporated milk*
- *2 (6-ounce) packages frozen coconut (or fresh coconut may be used - 12 ounces)*
- *Reserve some coconut*

Mix sugar, salt and flour in skillet. Blend in milk. Cook over medium heat, stirring until thickened. Cool slightly. Stir in coconut. Spread between layers. Ice cake with seven-minute frosting. Sprinkle top with some coconut you have reserved. Refrigerate if kept overnight. —*Anne Seagraves, Clarke County, Georgia*

Family Wedding and Anniversary photos, bottom row, L-R: Annie D and Petie Seagraves, Billy and Jo Dobbins Seagraves, Ed and Myrtis Dobbins; Annie D and Petie Seagraves' at their 50th Anniversary party, Jessie Mae Fields, Jimmy and Mary Seagraves Fields, Annie D and Petie Seagraves, Phillip Seagraves. Top row, L-R: Rebecca Seagraves Baugh and Herman Baugh, Phillip and Donny Bailey Seagraves with Phillip's uncle Rev. Gene Pettyjohn officiating, and Petie Seagraves beside Phillip; Lori Fields Loden and Gary Loden.

Chapter 16

Christmas at the Seagraves House

Christmas was always a busy time in the Seagraves household. Mother, Reba Winn Seagraves, was from the school of "everything had to be cleaned from top to bottom." Walls had to be washed and screens cleaned. Furniture had to be moved and cleaned from top to bottom. Pictures, mirrors, vases, etc., were washed. Shades were taken down and thoroughly cleaned. Floors were cleaned by mopping and waxing. Nothing escaped its thorough cleaning, including china cabinets, closets, beds, and bedding.

Invariably when all of this was completed on Christmas Eve night, when we were getting ready for bed, the bathroom kerosene heater would start smoking and cause Mother great concern and extra cleaning.

Baking was begun early. Japanese fruitcake, lemon cheesecake, fresh cocoanut cake, caramel cake, chocolate cake, pound cake, and fruitcake were offered for our Christmas feasting. Homemade candies, usually including divinity and chocolate fudge, store-bought hard candies, chocolate drops, chocolate-covered cherries, etc., were in plentiful supply. Fruits and nuts were also a part of our Christmas bounty.

Harvey Lee "Bob" and Reba Winn Seagraves in front of their Athens, Georgia house—From Hope Seagraves Austin

My sister Barbara and I would be instructed to seat all of our dolls on the sofa for Santa to see. If they were in "good" condition, Santa would leave us a new doll for Christmas. Getting our dolls ready for Santa's inspection included washing their clothes (Mother or our maid ironed them). We cleaned their faces, etc., with Mother's cold cream. They were seated on the sofa on Christmas Eve, waiting for Santa to see them. By the way, I still have several of my dolls with their original outfits.

Fireworks were plentiful. My father liked Roman candles, which he'd light. Firecrackers, sparklers, cherry bombs, and "son-of-a-guns" were part of the Seagraves' noisy celebration.

We children were always involved in the Christmas play at church —girls were usually angels, and the boys were shepherds (bathrobes and towels on their heads as their costumes). Girls wore white robes with tinsel halos and sometimes wings, usually appearing in the baptismal pool on a platform behind the choir and above the pulpit area (our stage).

Santa was generous to us on Christmas. We usually were given our most wanted gift. When Barbara and I were older, probably 8 and 10, we were told we could go to Athens Sporting Goods and choose a bicycle that we would like to have, but that we would probably receive only one of them at Christmas. Barbara was smaller and younger, and she chose a blue girl's bike with balloon tires. I chose a smaller tire larger navy blue bike. I knew in my heart that we would receive the bike Barbara had chosen because my choice would be too big for her. Imagine our happiness and joy when we entered the living room on Christmas morning and found both bikes waiting for us!

Bubble lights on a Seagraves Christmas tree

Hours, very enjoyable ones, were spent riding those bikes all over the university campus, especially River Road, where we usually stopped by the grave of someone's dog and paid our respects. The university's trash pile for paper was located on the road, and after we learned about it from our friends (both boys and girls), we would stop by and choose crepe paper which had been used as decorations and decorate our bike spokes.

Seagraves family members gathered for an event. Front row, L-R: Harvey Lee "Bob" Seagraves, Reba Winn Seagraves. Back row, L-R: Gaynelle Seagraves Farr Wansley, Rebecca Seagraves Baugh, Barbara Seagraves Tiller Carter.—From Hope Seagraves Austin

We rode miles on dirt roads. East Campus Road and River Road were two of our favorites. Oconee Hills Cemetery was another of our favorite riding spots. We often rode our bikes to Mr. (Jim) Smith's mausoleum. We had been told that if you asked him what he was doing, he would answer, "nothing." On a particular day, we asked the question, and the wind became gusty and rattled the windows. We made record time getting out of the cemetery that day.

Having been born the sixth child of my Father (my Mother's eldest), we were blessed with a large family gathering, especially at Christmas. Mother cooked for the whole family. When Barbara and I were older, we assisted as Mother directed. We usually had a large fresh ham which Mother had cooked all night on Christmas Eve. (Some of this ham was part of our Christmas breakfast with eggs, biscuits, and butter). Mother served milk from her cows (one or more), and we also had hot chocolate, fresh orange juice, homemade jelly, preserves, or jam.

Dinner, about two or three o'clock on Christmas Day, consisted of turkey (many times bought in Madison County from some of Mother's relatives) or several big hens (often raised in our yard by Mother and Daddy), onion cornbread dressing, green beans, potato salad, candied sweet potatoes, cranberry sauce, pickles — often peach pickles put up by Mother, butter, homemade biscuits, cornbread, and iced tea. Our usual beverage was milk — sweet or buttermilk. Desserts included the variety of cakes Mother baked and homemade ambrosia made with fresh oranges and fresh coconut. Candy was also available.

Since all of us couldn't eat at the dining room or kitchen table, the men and boys ate first. We women and girls waited on the tables, washed the dishes, and then ate after replenishing the tables. The men sat around and visited while the dishes were washed, dried, and put away. Mother took care of the leftovers if there were any remaining. This tradition continued as long as my father, H. L. (Bob) Seagraves, lived.

Presents under the tree on a long-ago Christmas in Phillip and Donny Bailey Seagraves' Winterville home. Two family members who enjoyed eating a Christmas meal and opening presents with us that year in this house were Rebecca Seagraves Baugh and her husband Herman Baugh.

Mother's family — Barbara, Goss, and their three daughters, Donald and Melissa, and their son and daughter, David and Trixie, and their two children, a daughter and son continued to come to Athens to Mother's house for Christmas Dinner. After Mother became disabled with rheumatoid arthritis and the beginning of Parkinsonism, the family shifted to our house for Christmas. On Mother's last Christmas with us (December 1985), we realized it would probably be her last one. Barbara suggested the family get together under one roof for a long weekend of visiting, eating, playing, and sleeping. This we continued to do.

God has blessed us, and we are trying to honor Him and our Mother's request that we continue to get together as a family. She strove to make sure that all of her children and their children know one another and not gather only for funerals, but also for happy times as well.—Rebecca Seagraves Baugh

---

This article was written by Rebecca Seagraves Baugh, a retired teacher and guidance counselor, for a December 1996 special edition of *The Thumb Tack Tribune,* which once was the Athens High School newspaper. Rebecca was the oldest daughter of Harvey Lee "Bob" Seagraves and his second wife, Reba Winn Seagraves. Her grandparents were Hardy Calloway Seagraves and Pink Carithers Seagraves. She was a sister of Gaynelle Seagraves Farr Wansley, Harvey Hill "Sleepy" Seagraves, Frank Ed Seagraves, Nelson "Petie" Seagraves, Harold Seagraves, Barbara Seagraves Tiller Carter, Donald Winn Seagraves and David Hartford Seagraves. When this book was written, only David Hartford Seagraves was still living.

Chapter 17

Pettyjohn Family History

Luke Pettyjohn, son of William and Ethel Pettyjohn, researched and wrote the following Pettyjohn family history article with his wife, Mabel Farr Pettyjohn, from Luke's point of view, in the days before the internet and sites like ancestry.com existed. Luke and Mabel visited libraries and traveled to many places mentioned in this article to talk to relatives and do their family history research.

Luke and Mabel's Pettyjohn Family History

As I stood at the foot of Pigeon Mountain, with its steep slopes towering above, I wondered how my parents could have left this land on which four generations of Pettyjohns had lived. Pigeon Mountain is a spur of Lookout Mountain, located in northwest Georgia in Walker County. It was named for the passenger pigeon, which roosted here in the thousands before its extinction.

Pigeon Mountain in Walker County, Georgia, where many Pettyjohn ancestors lived and are buried. This photo was taken from the yard of the Chattoga Baptist Church in LaFayette, Georgia.—From Rev. Eugene "Gene" Pettyjohn

This land is now part of the 4,200 acres owned by the National Forest Service in order to preserve its primitive beauty and wild animals. On my ancestors' original land is located Pettyjohn's Cave, of which four and one-half miles have been mapped.

Jacob Pettyjohn and John Bankston

My third great-grandfather, Jacob Pettyjohn of Virginia, had fought in the Revolutionary War and, after the war, in the mid-1780s, had been given several grants of land in Wilkes and Warren counties. At the same time, another great-great-great-grandfather, John Bankston (sometimes spelled Banksten), had also been granted land in these counties.

About 1800, both men moved to Jackson County, and in the early 1830s, their sons moved to Walker County, where at that time, it was known as the Cherokee Lands.

This charcoal portrait of Jacob W. and Sarah Bankston Pettyjohn is still in the family. Jacob served in the Civil War, Company I, 60th Georgia Infantry as a Private. He was captured in Winchester, Virginia on September 19, 1864.—Photo by Donny Bailey Seagraves

Mary Etta Srite Pettyjohn (07-24-1860 - 10-26-1929) and her husband Joseph A. Pettyjohn (01-25-1861 - 01-03-1920)—From Wayne Pettyjohn

Jacob Pettyjohn's son, Abraham, in the 1832 Land Lottery, had drawn one hundred and sixty acres at the foot of Pigeon Mountain. Here his son, Jacob, had been born, and when a young man had married Sarah Bankston. To them had been born my grandfather, Joseph Pettyjohn.

Henry and Martha Pruitt Srite, parents of Mary Etta Srite Pettyjohn—From Luke Pettyjohn

Pettyjohns on Top of Pigeon Mountain

Joseph, in the early 1880s, married my grandmother, Mary Etta Srite. Her grandparents had come to this part of Georgia in 1853, and in the nearby Fairview Cemetery, their tombstones read: "Mary N. Srite, daughter of Rev. Charles Hilton, born in East Tenn. June 2, 1802, married Jacob Srite Feb. 2, 1823, moved with him to Georgia in 1853, died Sept. 17, 1880."

Beside her is the grave of her husband: "Jacob Srite, born May 27, 1793, died Mar. 31, 1885." In this same cemetery are the ancestors of Joseph Pettyjohn buried as well.

Joseph and Mary Etta Srite Pettyjohn with their daughter and four of their sons. Front row, L-R: Enoch Alonzo "Lon," Joseph, Mary holding baby Thomas Watson "Tom." Back row, L-R: Twins William Ephraim "Will," and Henry Manassie and their sister Annie. The Pettyjohns' youngest son John had not yet been born when this photo was taken.

Joseph and Mary Etta, with their little daughter Annie, lived on top of Pigeon Mountain. One night, a tornado completely blew down their house, leaving only the high-backed headboard of the bed in which the three of them were sitting, with one wall of the house leaning against the headboard.

They went down into the valley to the home of a neighbor, and the next morning, April 2, 1884, my father, William Pettyjohn, and his twin brother, Henry, were born.

In the next few years, three more sons were born, making a total of one girl and five boys. (Note: In some genealogy books and family history websites, another son, Dewey L., is listed. We do not know his date of birth or death. He apparently died at birth or shortly after that.)

Pettyjohn Family Tree

Jacob Pettyjohn & Elizabeth Staton Pettyjohn

|

Abraham Pettyjohn & Mary "Polly" Rogers Pettyjohn

|

Jacob William Bate Pettyjohn & Sarah Ann Bankston Pettyjohn

|

Joseph A. "Nick" Pettyjohn & Mary Etta Srite Pettyjohn

|

William E. "Will" Pettyjohn & Cora Ethel Strickland Pettyjohn

|

Agnes Pettyjohn Russell, Willie Belle Pettyjohn Strickland, Simon Joseph Eugene "Gene" Pettyjohn, Waymon Victor "Vic" Pettyjohn, Anne "Annie D" Pettyjohn Seagraves, Luther "Luke" Pettyjohn, Mary E. Pettyjohn Norris Cape

Being Self Sufficient

Here's a double-barreled black powder shotgun, circa 1895, that has been handed down in the Pettyjohn family. It most likely belonged to Joseph Pettyjohn.—Photo by Phillip Seagraves

The Pettyjohn family was very self-sufficient, making their own soap, getting honey from their twelve beehives, making mattresses and pillows from the down of their geese, and also straw mattresses from threshed wheat, from which they also got "shorts" or whole grain flour.

Annie Pettyjohn Williams, Joseph and Mary Etta Pettyjohn's only daughter. Annie D Pettyjohn Seagraves is named after her aunt Annie.—From Bill Simmons

On their spinning wheel, they spun their cotton, and with a small knitting machine, Mary Etta knitted their sox. They had a canner about two by four feet on legs, underneath which was a small furnace. In the top was very hot water, into which they placed the cans.

They raised a few cows for beef and milk, and up on the mountain ranged their hogs during the summer, which in the winter were rounded up and killed, providing sausage and lard.

They had thirty-five or forty acres of peaches, which, when ripe, were picked in one day by laborers who also worked at nearby mines and loaded on boxcars to be shipped to Kentucky. From the boxcars, the family got ice, with which they made peach ice cream. They also made peach brandy for family use.

My grandfather owned a sawmill and cotton gin. These brought in needed cash, as did his blacksmithing for two of the nearby mines. He also made caskets. He was school board chairman and was in charge of paying the teachers' salaries, which were about $40 per month.

Stricklands and Coffmans

Simon Y. and Salina "Linia or Lina" Coffman Strickland, parents of Ethel Strickland Pettyjohn and her siblings, including Guthbert, Exa, Leona and Lela.—From Pettyjohn family photo albums

In 1850, my mother's father, Simon Y. Strickland, lived in this part of Georgia with an uncle, Hugh Wilson. His ancestors had come from North Carolina into Wilkes County in the late 1700s.

Shortly after marrying, he built a nice two-story house on the edge of what is now the Chickamauga National Battlefield Park, which today is standing and is in excellent condition. His name is mentioned several times in a book written by a Confederate nurse, referring to wounded soldiers in his home. After the war, he gave land for the Burning Bush Church and a school.

The Strickland family, front row, L-R: Cora Ethel Strickland Pettyjohn holding a book, her mother Salina "Linia" (sometimes spelled Lina) Coffman Strickland, Margaret Exa Strickland. Back row, L-R: Guthbert and Leona. Not pictured is older sister Katie Lela Wilson and brothers William Edward and Thomas Judson and two older half sisters, Mary Emma Strickland and Sarah Elizabeth Strickland.—From Luke Pettyjohn

In the early 1870s, his wife and oldest daughter died, and later, he moved into the area, about seven miles from the Pettyjohn family, where he met and married my grandmother, Lina Coffman, twenty-five years younger than he. Lina's ancestors, the Coffmans and Clarkes, had lived in East Tennessee since the late 1700s, and in 1850, her father, Andrew Coffman, had moved to this part of Georgia.

INFORMATION FROM THE STRICKLAND FAMILY BIBLE...Copied May 9, 1972

(BIRTHS)

Simon Y. Strickland was born Friday April 26, 1822
Tincy C. Dalton, wife of Simon Y Strickland was born July 25, 1834
Mary Emma Strickland was born January 7, 1857 (Wednesday)
Sarah Elizabeth Strickland was born September 6, 1865
Linia E. Coffman, wife of Simon Y Strickland was born February 7, 1847
Hatie Lela Strickland was born August 2, 1877
William Edward Strickland was born November 20, 1878
Thomas Judson Strickland was born January 26, 1881
Leona Strickland was born April 13, 188[illegible]
Cuthbert Y. Strickland was born September 30, 1884
Cora Ethel Strickland was born May 6, 1887
Margaret Exa Strickland was born July 11, 1890
Nora E Strickland was born October 21, 1893
Ollin Vandell Strickland was born January 12, 1912
Granvell E. Strickland was born March 2, 1914
Imogene E. Strickland was born February 27, 1916
Edron Dwight Strickland was born October 25, 1919
Margaret Lena Strickland was born December 25, 1921
Eddie Lavern Strickland was born January 28, 1924
J. C. Strickland was born May 17, 192[illegible]
Melba G. Strickland was born December 9, 1929
Jeanette D. Strickland was born August 10, 1930

Information from the Strickland Family Bible, copied May 9, 1972—From Anne Seagraves' papers

To Lina and Simon Strickland were born one son and four daughters, my mother, Ethel Strickland, being the third child. When she was eight, in 1895, her father died, and eight years later, in 1903, her mother passed away. The remaining children continued to live together, farming their land until 1910, when my mother and father married.

So it was here, at the foot of Pigeon Mountain, that Mama and Papa grew up, living about seven miles apart.

Rev. Gene Pettyjohn with Nora Strickland, an aunt he met on a visit to Walker County, Georgia to research family history. Like his brother Luke, Gene had a keen interest in tracing his family roots. —From Rev. Gene Pettyjohn

Uncle John, Papa's youngest brother, told me that "Will went with a girl named Fanny Mahan before he met Ethel. Everybody thought they were going to get married."

When I asked, "Why?" he replied, "Because they went together for almost six years."

When I inquired what had happened, he said, "The Mahans moved down in the lower part of the county."

From where Papa's family lived to the lower county line was only a matter of a few miles.

(MARRIAGES)

Simon Y. Strickland & Tincy C. Dalton were married October 17, 1850
John C. Hall & Mary E. Strickland were married August 17, 1874
Simon Y. Strickland MMMMMMMMMMM & Linia Coffman were married November 5,1876
H C Wilson & Lela Strickland were married August 2, 1896
William E Pettyjohn & Cora Ethel Strickland were married November 6, 1910
G. Y. Strickland & Nora Ethel Cagle were married January 22, 1911
Ervin L. Dorsey & Druey Leona Strickland were married September 9, 1911

(DEATHS)

Tincy C. Strickland (wife of S Y Strickland) Died May 29, 1871
Mary Emma Hall (daughter of S Y Strickland) died July 28, 1875
Thomas Judson Strickland died October 20, 1881
William Edward Strickland died November 1, 1881
Simon Y. Strickland died December 10, 1895
Linia C. Strickland (wife of S Y Strickland) died July 17, 1903
Leona (Strickland) Dorsey died July 4, 1919

PAGE # 2....STRICKLAND FAMILY RECORD.......(DEATHS) continued

Eddie Laverne Strickland (son of G Y & Nora Strickland) died June 14,1926
Guthbert Y Strickland died December 5, 1932
Margaret Exa Strickland died January 28, 1966
William E. Pettyjohn died May 24, 1962

Marriages and deaths copied from the Strickland Family Bible May 9, 1972—From Anne Seagraves' papers

William Pettyjohn's Younger Days

As a young man, Papa had worked at several jobs. For a while, he worked in an iron mine near Lafayette and later carried a Star Mail Route on a mule. A Star Route is not a regular mail route but is the delivering of mail out to smaller post offices. He also, at one time, did carpentry work, then blacksmithing, both of which he learned from his father.

William E. "Will" Pettyjohn as a young man in Walker County, Georgia—From Luke Pettyjohn

When about eighteen, he left home and went to Chattanooga, where he worked in a fruit and candy store. When the owner told him he could eat all he wanted, he thought he would never have enough and continually gorged himself, but eventually came to care nothing for either.

The Pettyjohn brothers, L-R: John, Lon, Will, Henry and Tom. Woman to the right is unidentified. This photo is from a Pettyjohn family reunion.

While living in Chattanooga, Papa heard the famous evangelists Billy Sunday and Gypsy Smith. He also went on an "excursion," a charter train trip to Pensacola, Florida, where the entire group boarded a boat in the Gulf of Mexico. Everyone was looking for fish. When a school of dolphins leaped, the entire crowd would rush from one side to the other, almost capsizing the ship. I have a memento Papa bought on his trip, a small container made of seashells, dated Pensacola, Florida, 1905.

Strangely, after being gone from home for two or three years,

Papa returned to Grandpa Pettyjohn's farm and remained there until 1910, when he and Mama married.

His twin brother, Henry, married a little before Papa did. It was said that Grandma Pettyjohn had picked out a wife for Uncle Henry, he being the most timid of her sons. Papa once said that an old widower who moved into their community asked Papa if he could help him get a wife. Papa answered that he had so much trouble finding a wife for himself that he would be of no help.

Will and Ethel Meet

Cora Ethel Strickland (Pettyjohn) at age 16—From Luke Pettyjohn

I do not know how Mama and Papa met. It might have been during a "protracted meeting," as "revivals" were called then, or perhaps at a music school since Papa knew how to sing the old "Fa, Sol, La," — three-note singing.

It could have been through one of Papa's younger brothers, Lon, who was courting Nora Cagle, a girl living on the adjoining farm to the Stricklands. It surprised me to learn that she had gone with Uncle Lon, and when I asked what had happened, she answered, "Lon was so terribly shy that Guthbert just jumped in and beat his time."

Lon Enoch Pettyjohn and his wife Mary Ruth Pettyjohn in a photo taken November 1964. They were the grandparents of Miriam Rushton.—From Miriam Rushton

I do not know if Fanny Mahan was too lively for Papa, but perhaps she was since he chose the opposite, Mama, who was shy and quiet. Uncle Lon, despite his shyness, married Ruth Surrett, and Aunt Ruth was by far the most talkative of the five Pettyjohn boys' wives, seeming to pause only to take a deep breath.

From L-R: Ethel Strickland Pettyjohn, Will Pettyjohn and Exa Strickland, Ethel's younger sister, circa 1920s or 1930s

Mama had gone with a boy named Julian Sizemore. His father, a preacher, had died, and he lived with his mother. I have a card from him to Mama in response to an invitation from her to some church social, saying he was sorry that he could not come home that weekend. He was then attending Mercer University and later became somewhat prominent in local Baptist circles. Mama always kept his picture and newspaper clippings about his activities.

Mama's oldest sister, Lela, ten years her senior, had married H. C. "Bud" Wilson in 1896, a few months after Grandpa Strickland died. Aunt Lela's oldest daughter was nine years younger than Mama, and later Mama's oldest children were the age of Aunt Lela's youngest. Mama and Aunt Lela looked almost like twins despite the ten-year age difference.

The same was true of Papa, who looked like he might have been the twin of his brother, Tom, ten years younger than he. However, Papa's twin brother, Henry, did not resemble Papa at all but looked quite a lot like Abraham Lincoln.

Fraternal twins, L-R: Henry Pettyjohn and William "Will" Pettyjohn

After the death of Grandma Linia Coffman Strickland in 1903, Mama's brother, Guthbert, Mama, and her other two sisters continued to live for seven more years on their farm until 1910. That year, Mama and Papa married on November 6; the following January, Guthbert and Nora Cagle married; and Mama's older sister Leona married in September – all marrying in less than one year. The youngest, Exa, never married and later worked in Chattanooga, coming home on the weekends to the old homeplace where Guthbert and Nora lived for the rest of their lives.

An antique Elgin sewing machine that belonged to Ethel Strickland Pettyjohn for many years and is still in the family. We believe they either brought it from Dalton, Georgia or bought it in Athens, Georgia after they moved there in 1933.—Photo by Phillip Seagraves

Mama and Papa went together for about two years. Once, when there had been a fair, a sewing machine was to be given away to any couple who would marry there, and many of their friends were asking if they would marry and get the free machine. It was probably the next fall before they married since neither of them was the type to be stampeded into any hasty action.

Marriage

The following letter was written by Papa to Mama two days before they married.

Friday, Nov. 4th, 1910

Miss Ethel Strickland,

My Dear Darling. How are you today? O.K, I hope. I am scared now (ha!). Say, Dear, I have made arrangements with Bro. Burk to administer the ceremony so will go over to his home. I will call about 1:15, and we will start as soon afterward as we well can.

I will close.

Yours to love evermore, W. E. P.

They were married November 6, 1910, at Naomi Church, a few miles east of Lafayette, in Walker County, by Rev. J. L. Burke, probably the same man who had been ordained and supported by Burning Bush Church, which had land given by Grandpa Strickland, who later attended that church.

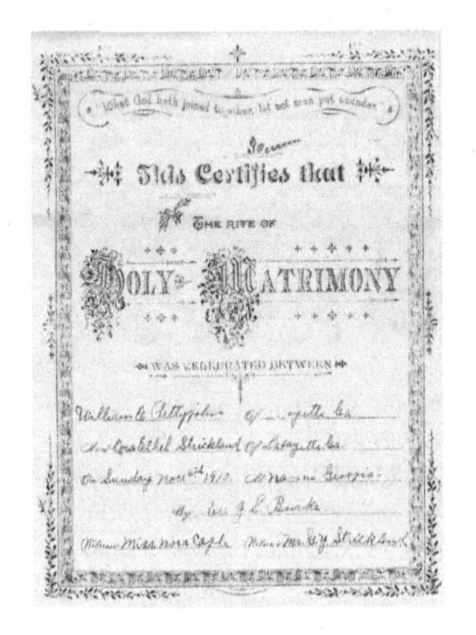

"What God hath joined together, let not man put asunder"

This Certifies that

The Rite of

Holy Matrimony

Was Celebrated Between

William E. Pettyjohn of ...ayette Ga

Miss Ethel Strickland of Lafayette Ga

On Sunday Nov 6th 1910 At Naomi Georgia

By Rev J L Burke

Witness Miss Nora Caple Witness Mr G. Y. Strickland

Will and Ethel Pettyjohn's marriage certificate

Mama and Papa lived on a farm with her older sister, Leona, and her husband, Edwin Dorsey, but shortly thereafter, Mama sold her interest in their old family farm to her brother, Guthbert, and she and Papa moved away.

The house in Walker County, Georgia where Annie D Pettyjohn Seagraves was born.

According to many of the old papers I have, Papa was always buying, selling, and moving from one place to another. Over a period of ten years, each of their seven children was born in a different house.

Anne "Annie D" Pettyjohn Seagraves in her second grade school picture, first row, 5th from the left. This school was most likely in Dalton, Georgia.

Working at Muscle Shoals

Luke Pettyjohn, author of this Pettyjohn family history article, along with his wife Mabel Farr Pettyjohn, on his "Green Hornet" scooter with daughter Carol Pettyjohn Hitt in the sidecar. Luke and his brother Gene both had a keen interest in Pettyjohn family history.—From Carol Pettyjohn Hitt

During World War I, in 1918 and early 1919, Grandpa Pettyjohn, Papa, and two of his brothers worked in Muscle Shoals, Alabama, where a dam was being built on the Tennessee River. Mama and her children lived with them for a while, Mama cooking for the group. After a short time, she tired of this and returned to Lafayette, and then Uncle Tom's wife went and did the cooking. The men would come home at least every other weekend until their work there was finished in Muscle Shoals.[1]

In some genealogical books and on some family history websites, there is information that says Jacob W. Pettyjohn, who was born in 1838 and died in 1892 in Walker County, Georgia, was adopted by Abraham Pettyjohn. Jacob's birth surname is listed as Bate. Luke and Mabel Pettyjohn did not include this information in their Pettyjohn family history article, and we do not know if it is accurate.

Jacob W. Pettyjohn's grave marker in Walker County, Georgia—
From Rev. Gene Pettyjohn

Chapter 18

The Pettyjohns Move to Athens, Georgia

Luke and Mable Pettyjohn ended their family history article in 1919, but there is more to the story.

We don't know exactly when Will and Ethel Pettyjohn and their children left their native town of LaFayette in Walker County, Georgia and moved to the town of Dalton in Whitfield County, about thirty miles away.

But we do know they were living in Dalton by 1921 because their youngest child, Mary Pettyjohn Norris Cape, was born there that year.

Pettyjohn family members in Dalton, Georgia circa 1920s, L-R: Ethel Pettyjohn, Anne "Annie D" Pettyjohn Seagraves, unknown, Mary Pettyjohn Norris Cape. Back row: Victor "Vic" Pettyjohn

Dalton, Georgia

Several textile mills were built in Dalton during the late 1800s, including the Crown Cotton Mill, near Hamilton's Spring in 1884, followed by the Elk Cotton Mill and the American Thread Mill south of town. In 1917, Chattanooga native G. Lamar Westcott, who had studied yarns and knitting procedures at the Philadelphia Textile Institution, established Dalton Hosiery Mills, later renamed Westcott Hosiery Mills.

Anne as a child in Dalton, Georgia. Front row, L-R: Mary Pettyjohn Norris Cape, unknown, Anne "Annie D" Pettyjohn Seagraves. Back row, L-R: Luke Pettyjohn, maybe Vic Pettyjohn

Will Pettyjohn found a job in one of these Dalton mills. In a 1930 U.S. Federal Census record, he lived in Dalton, Whitfield County. He owned his house, which was valued at $600 (about $10,193 today), could read and write and worked as a mechanic at a hosiery mill. Also listed were his wife Ethel, forty-two, and children: Agnes, eighteen, Willie (Belle), seventeen, Eugene, sixteen, Victor, fourteen, Annie, twelve, Luther, ten and May (Mary) E, nine.

Chenille Bedspreads

Not only was Dalton known as a textile center, it also was called the "Bedspread Center of the World." A young Dalton resident, Catherine Evans, later Whitener, revived the candlewick tradition of producing hand tufted bedspreads by tufting cotton yarns into muslin fabric. By the 1910s, others followed her lead, building a cottage industry of tufting at home.

> "As a young child, Catherine Evans Whitener from Dalton, Georgia, saw a candlewick bedspread, observing that strands of tufts (made of yarn) were pushed through fabric and then clipped, which produced a fuzzy look, just like a caterpillar. The tufting became known as "chenille," which is the French word for caterpillar. While many of the chenille bedspreads were sewn by hand, innovators altered their sewing machines to tuft. Chenille bedspreads roared in popularity, just like the infamous 1920s decade, and even survived the Great Depression."
>
> — Cottagedevine.com - Vintage Chenille Bedspreads: A Brief History

---

The Pettyjohn family would have seen these chenille bedspreads displayed and sold along the Dixie Highway, later Highway 41, which became known as Bedspread Boulevard or Peacock Alley (because of the popular and colorful Peacock design on many of the chenille bedspreads sold there).

A chenille bedspread made by William "Will" Pettyjohn in the popular peacock design—From Mary Seagraves Fields

Before they left Dalton, Will learned how to alter a sewing machine so he could make tufted chenille bedspreads. He brought this profitable "side hustle," as we call it today, with him when the Pettyjohn family moved to Athens, Georgia in 1933.[1]

The Great Depression

L-R: Eugene "Gene" Pettyjohn and Victor "Vic" Pettyjohn

The Great Depression began in 1929 and lasted through most of the 1930s. Times for families like the Pettyjohns were hard during the depression. By 1933, Will may have lost his job at the mill in Dalton and might have been unable to find other work in the area. He heard about a job opportunity at Rogers Hosiery Mill in Athens, Georgia, and moved his family there.

In 1933, Will was almost fifty years old, Ethel was forty-five, and the children were teenagers and young adults. It couldn't have been easy to pull up roots in Dalton and move to an unfamiliar town one hundred fifty miles away. Oldest daughter Agnes was already married to Morris Russell, a son of a country doctor related to Senator Richard B. Russell, and stayed behind in Dalton. Oldest son Gene, who could drive a car, also stayed in Dalton, joining the family in Athens the next year.

From L-R: Mary Pettyjohn Norris Cape, unnamed dog, Anne "Annie D" Pettyjohn Seagraves, sitting on the porch of a house in Dalton, Georgia

Athens, Georgia in the 1930s

When the Pettyjohn family moved to Athens, the classic city had a population of about 18,000 people. Sanford Stadium on the University of Georgia campus was only four years old, having opened for its first football game against Yale, in 1929. Driving down Prince Avenue, the family would have admired many beautiful columned homes, including the twin Michaels brothers' houses and the T.R.R. Cobb house. They also would have noted Athens General Hospital, which opened its doors in 1919 and is today Piedmont Athens Regional Medical Center.[2]

After working as a mechanic for Rogers Hosiery Mill, Will later found a similar job at Climax Hosiery Mill where Nelson "Petie"

Seagraves, the man who would later become Will's daughter Annie D's husband, also worked.

The Pettyjohn House on Boulevard

One of the early houses the Pettyjohn family bought and lived in was on Georgia Depot Street (later changed to Georgia Drive). They eventually sold that house to daughter Willie Belle and husband Ernest Strickland who lived there for several years with daughters Sharon, Margie and Patricia, before moving to Toccoa, Georgia in 1955.

Will and Ethel Pettyjohn's former house at 738 Boulevard—Photo taken in 2018 by Phillip Seagraves

After selling the Georgia Depot Street house, the Pettyjohns purchased a large house in what is now The Boulevard Historic District, which is roughly bounded on the south by Prince Avenue and on the west by Hiawassee Street, and on the north by the Seaboard Coastline Railroad (now CSX), and on the east by Pulaski Street.

Will and Ethel Pettyjohn on the steps of their Boulevard house.

In the 1940 U.S. Federal Census record, Will, fifty-six, is listed as owning the house at 738 Boulevard and its value is $2,000 (equivalent to about $40,530 dollars in 2022). Will worked as a mechanic and his salary was $1,000 (about $20,265 in 2022 dollars).

Others living in the Pettyjohn house in 1940 were: Cora (Ethel), fifty-two, Willis (Willie Belle), twenty-seven, Thomas (Luke), twenty,

Mary E Norris, nineteen, and her husband Constine (Cornelius) J. Norris, twenty-one.

Bottom row photos, L-R: Phillip Seagraves and Mark Russell on the steps of the Russell house in Dalton, Georgia; Mary Pettyjohn Norris Cape with son David; Agnes Pettyjohn Russell, Annie D Pettyjohn Seagraves, Willie Belle Pettyjohn Strickland, Mary Pettyjohn Norris Cape. Top row photos, L-R: June Pettyjohn Blackwell, Mike Pettyjohn, Mary Seagraves Fields, Billy Seagraves and behind them is their grandfather Will Pettyjohn; Billy Seagraves, Nelson "Petie" Seagraves, Mary Seagraves Fields; Mary Pettyjohn Norris Cape with son David Norris, Annie D Pettyjohn Seagraves with daughter Mary Seagraves Fields.

The former Pettyjohn house is on Boulevard, near the corner of Chase Street and the present day Heirloom Cafe. The land underneath the Heirloom Cafe parking lot once was part of the Pettyjohn property. Will built a smaller house on that part of his lot many years ago and later on this house was moved to nearby Winterville.

The Boulevard neighborhood, a streetcar suburb of Athens, dates back to the late 1800s and is named after Boulevard (originally named "The Boulevard"), its widest street, which runs east/west through this one hundred fifty acre district.

Will and Ethel Pettyjohn in the yard of their house on Boulevard

The neighborhood is laid out in a gridiron pattern on slightly rolling terrain behind the capital mansions on the north side of Prince Avenue. The residential district where the former Pettyjohn house is located consists mostly of late-nineteenth and early twentieth century houses built primarily for blue collar and middle-class families.

Today, the Boulevard Historic District is listed on the National Register of Historic Places and has been locally designated as a Historic District (October 4, 1988).[3]

Boulevard Historic District sign—Photo by Donny Bailey Seagraves

The Pettyjohn's former house on Boulevard was built in 1880, making it one of the early homes in the neighborhood. It is Queen Anne style and has a wide front porch, perfect for sitting and visiting. Inside, there is a huge middle hallway with generously-sized rooms on either side.

Bottom row, L-R: Floy Jordan Pettyjohn; front of Will and Ethel's house on Boulevard; Ethel Pettyjohn. Top row, L-R: Ethel and Will Pettyjohn; L-R: Billy Seagraves, Mary Seagraves Fields, June Pettyjohn Blackwell, David Norris; Annie D Pettyjohn Seagraves

Will and Ethel's grandson Phillip Seagraves remembers his grandmother playing piano in the big front parlor. "She used to read from her collection of *Reader's Digest* magazines in there, too," he said. "Grandmother Pettyjohn loved to read."

During World War II, Will and Ethel's daughters, Willie Belle Strickland, Anne "Annie D" Seagraves and Mary Norris (later Cape), and daughter-in-law Floy Jordan Pettyjohn, moved into the Boulevard House, along with their children, while their husbands were away at war.

Nelson "Petie" Seagraves' Wartime Letter

Nelson "Petie" Seagraves' portrait from WWII

Here's a letter written by Annie D's husband Nelson "Petie" Seagraves to his Pettyjohn in-laws, Will and Ethel, while he was stationed in Germany, serving as a U.S. Army medic during World War II.

Thursday night, April 12, 1945

Dear Mom & Dad Pettyjohn,

Received your letter the other day, sure was glad to hear from you. Was so glad to hear that all of you were well and doing fine. I guess I can say the same only I haven't got my loved ones with me. But maybe the day isn't so far off now until I come to see them again.

Well, I guess you already know that I am in Germany. I can tell you one thing, I sure was surprised about this country because it sure is a pretty country. I just don't understand why those people always want to fight because looks like to me they have enough land here for all they need. But I guess long as there is a Germany, they will want to have war. But I don't believe they will ever have the chance again to start a war because there won't be any more (wars) when these GIs get through with them this time.

Well, you say you all are planting a (Victory) garden. Boy, I hope I get back in time to enjoy some of that good, fresh food right out of the garden. I know it will be real good. I guess I will sign off for now. All of you take good care of yourselves till I see you.

— Love to all, PFC Nelson "Petie" Seagraves

~

More Pettyjohns Move to Boulevard Neighborhood

Vic and Floy Pettyjohn's former house on Boulevard, next to Vic's parents Will and Ethel's former house—Photo taken in 2022 by Donny Bailey Seagraves

For a while, Gene and Nell Pettyjohn and their son Wayne lived in a house that no longer exists, on the right, looking from the street, next to Gene's Pettyjohn parents' house. Another son, Vic, and his wife

Floy Jordan Pettyjohn, bought the house to the left of Will and Ethel's house, looking from the street, and lived there for many years with their son Mike.

Mary Pettyjohn Norris, husband Cornelius and their three sons: David, Tommy and Steve, lived in this house on Boulevard, across the street from Mary's parents, Will and Ethel Pettyjohn.—Photo taken in 2022 by Donny Bailey Seagraves

The Pettyjohn's youngest daughter, Mary Pettyjohn Norris (later Cape), and her husband Cornelius, bought a house across the street and raised their three sons, David, Tommy and Steve, there. The Norris brothers have fond memories of living near their maternal grandparents, uncle, aunt and cousins.

Will Pettyjohn passed away in 1962 at age seventy-eight. Ethel continued to live in the Boulevard house, dying in 1981 at age ninety-four. The Pettyjohn family homeplace stayed in the family for many years after Will and Ethel died. Vic and Floy Pettyjohn's son, Mike, was the last family member to live there. In 2011, Daniel Epting bought the house, restored it and moved there with his family. The Epting family still lived in Will and Ethel Pettyjohn's former home in 2022.

A family portrait taken at Will and Ethel Pettyjohn's 50th Wedding Anniversary. Front row, L-R: Mark Russell, Steve Norris, Phillip Seagraves. Second row, L-R: Patricia "Trisha" Strickland Seabolt (who passed away in 2020), Carol Pettyjohn Hitt, Anne "Annie D" Pettyjohn Seagraves, Will Pettyjohn, Ethel Strickland Pettyjohn, Mary Pettyjohn Norris Cape, Margie Strickland Ward, Third row, L-R: Sharon Strickland Farmer, Agnes Pettyjohn Russell, Willie Belle Pettyjohn Strickland, Gene Pettyjohn, Floy Jordan Pettyjohn, Gaynelle Thaxton Norris, David Norris, Mary Seagraves Fields. Fourth row, L-R: Nelson "Petie" Seagraves, Morris Russell, Mabel Farr Pettyjohn, Luke Pettyjohn, Ernest Strickland, Cornelius Norris, Vic Pettyjohn, Jimmy Fields.

Chapter 19

Will and Ethel's Children

Will and Ethel Pettyjohn were the parents of seven children: Agnes Pettyjohn Russell, Rev. Eugene "Gene" Pettyjohn, Waymon Victor "Vic" Pettyjohn, Willie Belle Pettyjohn Strickland, Anne "Annie D" Pettyjohn Seagraves, Thomas Luther "Luke" Pettyjohn and Mary Pettyjohn Norris Cape.

The Pettyjohns were a close family and, for many years, got together at the house on Boulevard on Sunday afternoons. Will and Ethel enjoyed welcoming their children's spouses, grandchildren, and great-grandchildren into the family during their fifty-plus years of marriage.

Will and Ethel's descendants work in almost every profession and field imaginable today. Some Pettyjohn descendants still live in the Athens, Georgia area and enjoy cruising down the wide, still-beautiful street named Boulevard and remembering the good times they had there.

Read on for more information about Will and Ethel Pettyjohn's children.

Pettyjohn siblings and their spouses, L-R: Luke and Mable Pettyjohn, Ernest and Willie Belle Strickland, Nelson "Petie" and Anne "Annie D" Seagraves, Vic and Floy Pettyjohn, Cornelius and Mary Norris. Not pictured: Morris and Agnes Pettyjohn Russell, Rev. Gene and Nell Pettyjohn.

Agnes Pettyjohn Russell

Agnes Pettyjohn Russell, born August 9, 1911, in Walker County, Georgia, was Will and Ethel's oldest child. When the family moved from Dalton, Georgia, to Athens, Georgia, in 1933, Agnes was already married and stayed behind with husband Morris Russell.

Morris and Agnes Pettyjohn Russell with their son Mark

Agnes and Morris were the parents of one child, Mark Russell. At the time this book was written, Mark still lived in the family home in Dalton. Agnes passed away November 4, 1978, at age sixty-seven.

Willie Belle Pettyjohn Strickland

Ernest and Willie Belle Pettyjohn Strickland

Willie Belle Pettyjohn Strickland, Will and Ethel's next oldest daughter was born December 14, 1912, in Walker County, Georgia. She moved to Athens, Georgia, with her family in 1933 and later married Ernest Strickland. Willie Belle and Ernest were the parents of Sharon Strickland Farmer, Margie Strickland Ward and Patricia Strickland Seabolt. Willie Belle died September 20, 2008. She was ninety-six years old.

Rev. Simon Joseph Eugene "Gene" Pettyjohn

Rev. Eugene "Gene" Pettyjohn was born on February 24, 1914, in Walker County, Georgia, and was Will and Ethel Pettyjohn's oldest son. He married Edith Nell White, and they were the parents of Wayne Pettyjohn.

Gene worked many years as a mail carrier for the Athens Post Office and also served as a Baptist pastor at several area churches. Gene died September 30, 2001, at age eighty-seven.

Rev. Eugene "Gene" Pettyjohn with his wife Nell White Pettyjohn

Waymon Victor "Vic" Pettyjohn

Victor "Vic" and Floy Jordan Pettyjohn

Waymon Victor "Vic" Pettyjohn, next oldest son of Will and Ethel, was born in Walker County, Georgia, on October 14, 1915. He married Floy Frances Jordan, and they were the parents of June Pettyjohn Blackwell and Michael "Mike" Pettyjohn.

Vic worked for many years as a mail carrier for the Athens Post Office. He died October 22, 2003, at age eighty-eight.

Exa Annie Derrell "Annie D" Pettyjohn Seagraves

Nelson "Petie" and Anne Pettyjohn Seagraves

Anne "Annie D" Pettyjohn Seagraves, a daughter of Will and Ethel, was born August 3, 1917, in Walker County, Georgia. She married Nelson "Petie" Seagraves, and they were the parents of William

"Billy" Seagraves, Mary Seagraves Fields and Phillip Seagraves. Anne died on January 16, 2006, at age eighty-eight.

Thomas Luther "Luke" Pettyjohn

Luther "Luke" Pettyjohn, Will and Ethel's youngest son, was born October 23, 1919, in Walker County, Georgia. He married Mable Virginia Farr, and they were the parents of Carol Pettyjohn Hitt. Luke moved with his family from Dalton, Georgia, to Athens, Georgia, in 1933.

Luke and Mable Farr Pettyjohn—From Norris family albums

He worked as a mail carrier for the Athens Post Office for many years and retired to the North Georgia mountains. Luke died in 2009 at age ninety and is buried in Marble Hill, Pickens County, Georgia.

Mary Elizabeth Pettyjohn Norris Cape

Cornelius and Mary Pettyjohn Norris—From Norris Family Albums

Mary Pettyjohn Norris Cape, the youngest daughter of Will and Ethel, was born March 18, 1921, in Whitfield County, Georgia. She moved with the family to Athens, Georgia, in 1933. Mary married Cornelius Norris, and they were the parents of David, Tommy and Steve.

After the death of her first husband, Mary married Eucalee Cape. Mary died at age eighty-eight on January 19, 2010.

Will and Ethel Pettyjohn celebrated their 50th wedding anniversary with their children. Front row, L-R: Agnes Pettyjohn Russell, Will Pettyjohn, Ethel Strickland Pettyjohn, Mary Pettyjohn Norris Cape, Vic Pettyjohn. Back row, L-R: Luke Pettyjohn, Willie Belle Pettyjohn Strickland, Anne "Annie D" Pettyjohn Seagraves, Rev. Gene Pettyjohn.

Chapter 20

Cookies

Mary Seagraves Fields: Feels Like Home Again

Mary Seagraves Fields surveyed the rolling acres surrounding her old farmhouse in rural Jackson County, Georgia. "It feels like home again," she said. "I always hoped I'd get back home someday and maybe even have a chicken farm again, but I never dreamed it would be here."

"Here" is the same house and chicken farm Mary left seven years ago when she and her three children moved to Atlanta. They wanted a different life from what they'd known on the farm. No more picking up eggs twice a day, seven days a week. No more driving ten miles or more for shopping. No more cackle, cackle of chickens in the background of their lives. They were ready to get out of the country, meet new people, and experience all the benefits a city like Atlanta could offer.

So they sold the farm with its rolling acres, quaint old farmhouse, and income-generating chicken operation. Mary even financed part of the deal for the eager buyer. Then they purchased an attractive suburban home in Mableton, near Atlanta, and became city slickers.

Mary Seagraves Fields' former farmhouse on Brock Road in Jackson County, Georgia—Photo by Donny Bailey Seagraves

For seven years after that, I only saw them on brief visits, holidays and occasional weekends. Soon the children were children no longer. One got married, one graduated from high school, and the youngest was now a handsome young man of fifteen.

Several times during the past seven years, I heard Mary say wistfully: "I really wish I could move back here. I'd like to be home again. But I just don't know how to work it out."

Someone must have been listening to Mary because a few weeks ago, she received word that her farm was coming back to her; the buyer had defaulted on his loan and deserted the property.

It was a sad, lonely place littered with trash and the filth of desperate people when Mary visited the farm after receiving the notice. Rusty junk cars dotted the landscape. The once lovely farmhouse overflowed with what looked like debris from a county dump. Down the hill in the deserted chicken house, they found one solitary

Visiting at Mary Seagraves Fields' Jackson County farm. First row, L-R: Anne "Annie D" Pettyjohn Seagraves, Jen Seagraves, Donny Bailey Seagraves, Phillip Seagraves. Back row, L-R: Travis Fields, Mary Seagraves Fields, Kevin Fields, Greg Seagraves, Mike Bailey.

chicken, a scrawny survivor, presiding over the rusting, stinking remains of a once-thriving egg-laying house.

Now Mary had a hard decision to make: Should she take back the farm or just let it go? And if she took it back, could she turn it back into the place she'd left seven years ago, or was it beyond repair?

In the barn, Mary's daughter Lori found the name of her beloved horse, Patches, painted in her childish handwriting on the rough wooden wall. The horse had been left behind for the new owners to enjoy since there was no room for him in Atlanta. Now Patches was nowhere to be found. This wasn't the same peaceful place they'd left seven years ago. Even so, the basic parts were there: House, barn, the chicken house.

From L-R: Lori Fields Loden, Greg Seagraves, Jen Seagraves—Photo by Donny Bailey Seagraves

Mary prayed. Then she took the farm back.

A few weeks and many hours of back-breaking labor later, Mary sat in the kitchen of her farmhouse, surrounded by memories, both good and bad, drinking coffee, just as she had so many years before. The fire blazed and crackled in the ancient kitchen fireplace. Above the fireplace hung the oak-framed picture of a weathered old man, his hands clasped together, his head bowed in prayer. I remembered seeing that picture in the house years ago when I visited my sister-in-law.

"I don't know how, but I think we'll make it," Mary said. She sipped more steaming coffee and surveyed the kitchen and the gigantic living room beyond. "We've got a long way to go. But at least we're back home again."[1]

L-R: Travis Fields, Lori Fields Loden, Kevin Fields with their mother Mary Seagraves Fields—From Mary Seagraves Fields

Tea Cakes

- *3 pints flour*
- *1 cup* Crisco *or another shortening*
- *3 teaspoons soda*
- *1 teaspoon vanilla*
- *1/2 cup sweet milk*
- *3 eggs*
- *2 cups sugar*
- *6 teaspoons cream of tartar*
- *1 teaspoon salt*

Beat eggs. Add sugar, milk and vanilla. Sift flour in bowl. Add salt, cream of tartar and soda. Cut Crisco in. Now mix egg mixture with flour. Roll very thin, cut and cook on greased cookie pan until brown. —*Anne Seagraves, Clarke County, Georgia*

Ethel Pettyjohn's Sellers kitchen cabinet from her kitchen on Boulevard is still in the family. The Pettyjohn's bought this cabinet from a furniture store in Athens, Georgia, most likely in the 1930s.—Photo by Donny Bailey Seagraves

Grandmama's Tea Cakes

- *1/2 cup butter or margarine*
- *1/2 cup sugar*
- *1 egg (beaten)*
- *1 teaspoon vanilla*
- *1 cup (sifted) flour*

Cream butter and sugar. Add egg and vanilla, beating well. Blend in flour. Drop from teaspoon onto greased baking sheet, two inches apart. Bake in 350-degree oven ten to twelve minutes. Makes two dozen.—Ethel Pettyjohn, Clarke County, Georgia

Chocolate Chip Cookies

- *1 package Duncan Hines Deluxe II white cake mix (or any other brand)*
- *1/4 cup light brown sugar*
- *1 cup (6-ounce package) semi-sweet chocolate chips*
- *1/2 cup chopped nuts*
- *3/4 cup oil*
- *1 egg*

Preheat oven to 375 degrees. In a large bowl, stir all ingredients together until well-mixed. Drop from a teaspoon onto an ungreased cookie sheet. Bake at 375 degrees for ten to twelve minutes until cookies are golden brown (edges will look darker). Cool on cookie sheet for about one minute, then remove to rack to finish cooling. Makes about three and one-half dozen two-and-a-half-inch cookies. *—Mary Seagraves Fields, Jackson County, Georgia*

Chocolate Chip Oatmeal Drop Cookies

- *2 cups white sugar*
- *4 tablespoons cocoa powder*
- *1 stick margarine*
- *1/2 cup milk*
- *2 1/2 cups minute oatmeal*
- *1/2 cup peanut butter*
- *2 teaspoons vanilla extract*

Mix sugar, cocoa, margarine. Stir in one-half cup of milk. Cook in boiler over moderate heat only until you observe full boil. Remove from heat and add peanut butter and vanilla. Stir and allow mixture to cool slightly. Using a tablespoon, drop onto waxed paper, then allow cookies to cool. Ready to serve.—*Ann Seagraves, Madison County, Georgia*

Peanut Butter Cookies

- *1 cup shortening*
- *1 cup peanut butter*
- *1 cup white sugar*
- *1 cup brown sugar (fully packed)*
- *2 eggs*
- *1 teaspoon vanilla*
- *2 1/2 cups flour*
- *1/2 teaspoon salt*
- *3/4 teaspoon baking soda*
- *1/2 teaspoon baking powder*

Beat shortening and peanut butter together until creamy. Gradually add white sugar and brown sugar (fully packed), beating again. Then beat in eggs and vanilla. Then sift together flour, salt, baking soda and baking powder. Stir into peanut butter mixture.

Shape dough into one-inch balls. Place about two inches apart on an ungreased baking sheet. Flatten each by pressing crisscross with a fork. Bake in preheated oven 375 degrees for ten or fifteen minutes or until lightly browned. Remove from cookie sheet while still warm. —*Anne Seagraves, Clarke County, Georgia*

Bottom row, L-R: Albert and Margie Strickland Ward with their daughter Tracie Ward Wheeless; Luke Pettyjohn; Wayne Pettyjohn. Top row, L-R: One of Will and Ethel Pettyjohn's War Bond Books; Agnes Pettyjohn Russell in her fur coat; Rev. Gene Pettyjohn visiting the Holy Land.

Goof Balls

- *2 cups oatmeal*
- *1 cup peanut butter*
- *1/2 cup raisins*
- *1/2 cup wheat germ*

Mix all together and roll into balls. Let's set for a few minutes.—*Anne Seagraves, Clarke County, Georgia*

Just Cookies

- *2 sticks butter or margarine*
- *1 cup sugar*
- *1 cup chopped nuts*
- *2 cups flour*
- *2 teaspoons cinnamon*
- *1 egg yolk - save the white*

Mix all ingredients. Grease baking sheet. After ingredients are mixed and on baking sheet, spread egg white over top and sprinkle nuts on the top. Cook twenty-five minutes at 250 degrees. Cut into squares while hot.—*Anne Seagraves, Clarke County, Georgia*

Fruitcake Cookies

- *1/2 cup butter*
- *1 cup sugar*
- *2 eggs (beaten)*
- *1 1/2 cups plain flour*
- *3 1/2 cups pecans (broken)*
- *1 cup red candied cherries (chopped)*
- *2 slices candied pineapple (chopped)*
- *1/2 pound raisins*
- *1 cup dates (chopped)*
- *1/4 cup sweet milk*
- *1/2 teaspoon soda*
- *1/2 teaspoon cinnamon*

Cream butter and sugar. Add beaten eggs. Add all other ingredients and drop on greased cookie sheets. Bake in 300-degree oven until brown. Add two cups flour (rather than one and one-half cups), if you don't have raisins.—*Anne Seagraves, Clarke County, Georgia*

Sarah and Jacob Pettyjohn, Ancestors on the Wall

Jacob and Sarah Bankston Pettyjohn—Photo by Donny Bailey Seagraves

Jacob and Sarah Pettyjohn had been hanging on our wall for years, hidden behind a drawing of our former business, Seagraves Antiques, done for us as a Christmas gift by my aunt, Judith Coile Donohoe. When we were first married, the charcoal portrait of husband Phillip's long-forgotten ancestors occupied a place of honor in our living room, right above our TV.

One day I noticed, as Phillip and I lounged together on the couch, watching TV and laughing, Sarah and Jacob staring at us with antiquated disapproval shining from their pale, charcoal-colored eyes.

What are they trying to tell us? Do they think it's sinful for Phillip, their great-great-grandson, to sit here, laughing at a noisy box when he should be outside, plowing the fields or pounding red-hot iron into shoes for old Bessie the mule?

Whatever they were thinking, Sarah and Jacob looked, in their stuffy, high-collared, vintage clothing, as if they'd never laughed or even smiled, those two ancient, sour ghosts from

Phillip's past. Or maybe they were just tired of posing as they waited for the traveling artist to finish sketching them in charcoal.

Anyone looking at the portrait of Jacob and Sarah can see a definite family resemblance between Jacob and his great-great-grandson, Phillip. Jacob and Phillip have the same thick, dark hair and similar, slightly crooked noses. Phillip has some of Sarah in him, too – around the lips and in his inquiring eyes.

So why were Phillip's "kinfolk" covered by another picture? What caused us to hide them?

Blame it on my sister, Leanne. When she was a child, around the age of my 8-year-old twins now, she often spent the night at our house. One night, as Leanne was sleeping on the couch, she suddenly awoke from a terrifying nightmare to find Sarah and Jacob staring at her through the darkness. After that, Leanne claimed they were always watching her. She felt Sarah and Jacob's pale, faded eyes upon her everywhere in the house.

And so did I.

So Sarah and Jacob were covered, banished from view, even though we still knew they were there, and we could still feel them staring through the cheery, modern picture that hid them. They never complained; these pigmented people from Phillip's past, even though their beautiful, gilded frame displayed another picture over their ancient faces.

When Jenny and Greg learned we had exiled their ancestors behind another picture, they said, "When are you going to let us see our people?" And they kept asking until their dad uncovered Sarah and Jacob Pettyjohn, Greg and Jenny's great-great-great grandparents.

It was love at first sight as the children gazed at their charcoaled ancestors, and Sarah and Jacob gazed back at their twin descendants. Unlike their Aunt Leanne, Jenny and Greg loved having Sarah and Jacob beam down approvingly as their great-great-great grandchildren recited their multiplication tables and engaged themselves in a hot game of Uno. I guess one child's creepy ghosts can be another's long-lost ancestors.

Now, whenever I load the dishwasher, I feel Sarah's pale, disapproving gaze on my back. And as I pour myself another cup of coffee, I see Jacob's envious eyes focused on the aromatic steam rising from my mug.

Who knows? Maybe the ghosts of all of our ancestors are out there somewhere, staring at us as we go about our 20th-century lives full of modern, timesaving conveniences and devices. Maybe they are all watching us, these men and women, many of whom lived a hard, simple life as we live what they would surely consider a life of luxury.

Thank you, Jacob and Sarah, and the rest of our ancestors, for living your lives and making us and our way of life possible.[2]

Chapter 21

Pies

Annie D's Cousins

Anne "Annie D" Pettyjohn Seagraves used to talk about growing up in the North Georgia mountains and playing, along with her brothers, sisters and cousins, on Fort Mountain, which sits at 2,850 feet above sea level and is now a state park near Chatsworth, Georgia and the Cohutta Wilderness area. Two of those cousins were the Williams sisters, Rachel and Ruby.

Rachel Maryellen Williams Simmons

Annie D's cousin, Rachel Simmons, was born November 11, 1914, in Walker County, Georgia. Her parents were Charles and Annie Pettyjohn Williams. Rachel graduated from Chattanooga High School and McKenzie Business College. She worked at Crane Enamel Company, as executive secretary to Joe Engel at WDEF Radio and Engel Stadium, and as vice-president under her sister, Ruby Williams, at The Slim-Ez Company and R. B. Williams Co., Inc.

Rachel Maryellen Williams Simmons, Annie D's cousin—From Bill Simmons

Crowned Miss Lookout, Rachel loved fashion, modeling and beauty pageants. For years, she coached and assisted many young ladies in Miss Chattanooga, Miss Tennessee, Miss America and Miss USA pageants.

Rachel Simmons died January 12, 2022, at the age of 107.

> "Cousin Rachel was the daughter of Annie Pettyjohn Williams, the only sister of my grandfather, Lon Pettyjohn, and his brothers, including William "Will" Pettyjohn. Annie died at age thirty-four of tuberculosis. Her daughter Rachel lived in Chattanooga, on Missionary Ridge. I visited her there when she was 104 and found her to be delightful."
>
> — Miriam Rushton, Lon Pettyjohn's granddaughter

Ruby Williams

Ruby Williams, daughter of Charles and Annie Pettyjohn Williams and sister of Rachel Maryellen Williams Simmons, founded and, for many years, operated The Slim-Ez Company and R. B. Williams Co., Inc. Annie D enjoyed watching TV commercials for Ruby's Slim-Ez suit that supposedly made you lose weight when you exercised wearing it. She also watched Ruby when she appeared on the national television shows "What's My Line" and "To Tell the Truth." Ruby Williams, who once was awarded a U.S. Patent for a disposable waste system, lived until the age of 102.[1]

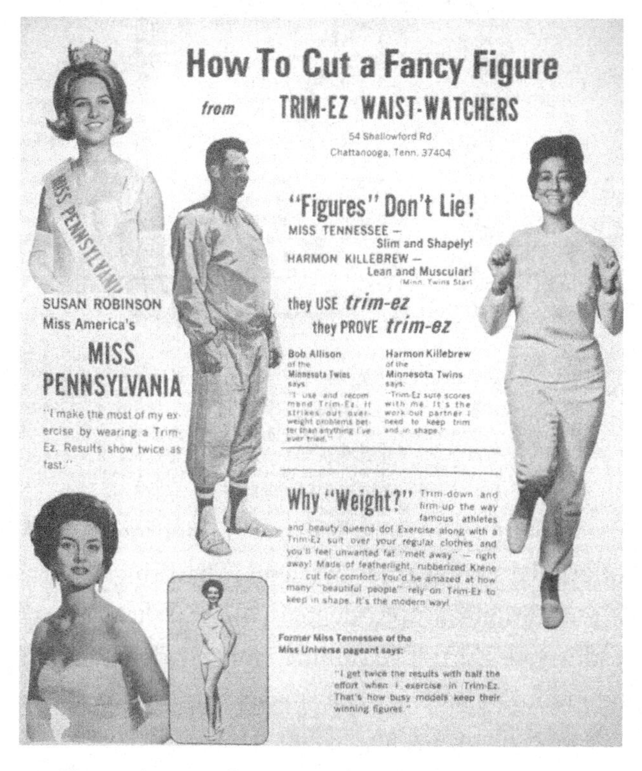

Here is a long ago advertisement for Ruby Williams' Trim-Ez Waist-Watchers sauna suit. The woman exercising in the suit, to the right, is Rachel Williams Simmons.—From Bill Simmons

Buttermilk Pie

- *3 eggs*
- *4 tablespoons flour*
- *2 cups buttermilk*
- *1 teaspoon lemon flavoring*
- *1 cup sugar*
- *1 tablespoon butter*
- *Grated rind of lemon*

Suzanne Seagraves Gerling with her daughter Meghan Gerling celebrating Suzanne's grandmother Anne "Annie D" Seagraves' 80th birthday at the Winterville, Georgia depot

Beat egg yolks and sugar. Mix flour and butter together. Add yolks, sugar, buttermilk, grated rind and lemon flavoring. Pour into crust and bake ten minutes at 450 degrees. Reduce heat to 350 degrees and bake thirty to thirty-five minutes longer. Beat egg whites until frothy and gradually add six tablespoons sugar. Spread over pie and brown.—*Anne Seagraves, Clarke County, Georgia*

Mrs. Turpin's Buttermilk Coconut Pie

- *1 1/2 cup sugar*
- *3 eggs*
- *1 tablespoon flour*
- *1/2 cup buttermilk*
- *1 stick butter (1/4 pound)*
- *1 can coconut*

Mix and pour in uncooked pie shell and cook at 325 degrees until done.—*Anne Seagraves, Clarke County, Georgia*

Three Strickland sisters, L-R: Ethel Strickland Pettyjohn, Lela Strickland Wilson and Exa Strickland, August 1955.

Aunt Exa's Butterscotch Pies

- *1/4 pound butter*
- *5 eggs*
- *3 cups sweet milk*
- *1/2 box brown sugar (dark)*
- *1 cup granulated sugar*

Whisk eggs lightly in a mixing bowl and set aside. Put butter and brown sugar in a vessel (saucepan) and brown them. Mix all ingredients, including the eggs, and cook until thick. Thicken with cornstarch and flavor to suit. Then put in pie crusts (baked).—*Exa Strickland (Ethel Pettyjohn's sister), Walker County, Georgia*

> "Ethel, I just use flour to thicken, and I put in a little salt to keep it from being so fresh. The recipe says it's for two, but it will make three pies if your pans aren't too large. Try them and write me how you like them. We sometimes sprinkle in a little coconut, too. Write me soon and tell me all the news."
>
> — Lovingly, Exa, (This extra information is from a note found with this recipe.)

Chess Lemon Pie

- *2 cups sugar*
- *1/4 cup sweet milk*
- *1 tablespoon cornmeal*
- *1/4 cup (melted) butter*
- *4 whole eggs*
- *1 tablespoon flour*
- *1/4 cup lemon juice*
- *2 teaspoons (grated) lemon rind*
- *2 unbaked pie shells*

Combine dry ingredients. Add to beaten eggs. Gradually add milk, melted butter, lemon juice and grated rind. Pour into unbaked pie shells and bake forty-five minutes at 350 degrees.—*Anne Seagraves, Clarke County, Georgia*

"All four Pettyjohn sisters were close. Anne and her younger sister Mary Pettyjohn Norris Cape were really close because they both lived in Athens most of their adult lives and they spent a lot of time together, especially in their older years. They visited us a lot at our house in Flowery Branch, Georgia. Steve and I loved seeing them sitting together on our deck, talking and laughing."

— Marcia Fair Norris, daughter-in-law of Mary Pettyjohn Norris Cape

---

Mary Pettyjohn Norris Cape and her older sister Anne "Annie D" Pettyjohn Seagraves—From Norris family photo albums

Chess Pie (Makes 2)

- *2 cups sugar*
- *1/4 pound butter*

- *1 tablespoon cornmeal*
- *1 tablespoon vanilla*
- *6 egg yolks (beaten)*
- *1 large can Pet (condensed) milk*
- *1 tablespoon flour*

Melt butter and add to sugar and beaten eggs. Cream until light. Add Pet condensed milk and dissolve thoroughly. Add flour, meal and vanilla and cream until light. Bake in two unbaked pie shells at 350 degrees for fifteen to twenty minutes.—*Anne Seagraves, Clarke County, Georgia*

Chocolate Pie

- *2 eggs*
- *3 teaspoons flour*
- *3/4 cup sugar*
- *Pinch of salt*
- *1 cup sweet milk*
- *1/3 cup cocoa*

Mix flour, sugar and cocoa. Beat eggs, then mix with flour mixture. Heat milk, then pour into mixture and cook until thick. Pour into baked pie shell. Add meringue if you wish. —*Anne Seagraves, Clarke County, Georgia*

Annie D with her younger sister Mary Pettyjohn Norris Cape at Anne's 80th birthday party at the Winterville Depot. This party was like a Pettyjohn family reunion and Anne loved that we got so many family members together to help celebrate her special day.—From Norris family photo albums

Chocolate Pie - Another Version

- *1 cup sugar*

- *5 tablespoons flour*
- *3 eggs (beaten yolks) - Save the whites*
- *1 teaspoon vanilla*
- *1 1/2 cups milk*
- *2 tablespoons butter*
- *1/4 cup cocoa*

Mix sugar, cocoa, flour and milk. Cook until thickened, then add well-beaten egg yolks. Cook two minutes longer, then remove from heat and add butter and vanilla. Pour into baked pie shell. Cover with meringue and bake thirty minutes at 325 degrees or until meringue is browned and set.—*Anne Seagraves, Clarke County, Georgia*

~

Our Annual Trip To Dalton, Georgia

Enjoying a picnic, L-R: Annie D Pettyjohn Seagraves, Ethel Pettyjohn, Nelson "Petie" Seagraves, Phillip Seagraves, Will Pettyjohn and Mary Seagraves Fields.

Each summer, when school let out, Grandpapa and Grandmama Pettyjohn, Mom (Annie D), sometimes my dad, my brother Billy and later on my brother Phillip and I (Mary E) loaded up Grandpapa's big, black car — I think it was a Dodge 4-door — for a trip to Dalton, Georgia to see Mom's older sister, Aunt Agnes Pettyjohn Russell, who stayed behind when the rest of our family moved to Athens in the 1930s.

Visiting at the Russell house in Dalton, Georgia. In front, Mark Russell holds a string of freshly-caught fish. Others in the photo: L-R: Phillip Seagraves, Petie Seagraves, unidentified, Will Pettyjohn, Agnes Pettyjohn Russell.

We usually stayed at Aunt Agnes and Uncle Morris' house a week. We would leave very early, before sunrise, because back in those days, we had no air conditioning in our cars, and it was too hot to be on the road in the middle of the day for a long trip.

Grandmama and Mom always packed good food and snacks for

the trip. About lunchtime, we stopped at a roadside park. Also, I think in Ellijay, on the side of the road in rock, was a pipe with the coolest, best-tasting spring water. Billy and I thought that was one of the best parts of our trip! These were really good times in long-ago days.—*Mary Seagraves Fields, Annie D's daughter*

Seagraves and Norris family members picnicking together. Bottom row, L-R: David Norris, Steve Norris, Mary Pettyjohn Norris (later Cape), Mary Seagraves Fields, Phillip Seagraves. Back row: L-R: Tommy Norris, Cornelius "Neely" Norris, Billy Seagraves, Anne Pettyjohn Seagraves—From Norris family photo albums

~

Foolproof Meringue

- *1 tablespoon cornstarch*
- *8 tablespoons sugar*
- *1/2 cup water*
- *3 egg whites with pinch of salt*

Mix cornstarch and two tablespoons of sugar with water and cook until clear, then set aside. Add pinch of salt to three egg whites and beat until foamy or standing in peaks, at which time you add the cornstarch mixture. Beat together until creamy, then add six tablespoons sugar gradually, beating well until very creamy. Pile on pie and bake thirty minutes at 325 degrees or until golden brown.—*Anne Seagraves, Clarke County, Georgia*

This photo is from a long ago Pettyjohn family reunion. Front row, L-R: Kelli Ward, Sharon Strickland Farmer, Phillip Seagraves, Nelson "Petie" Seagraves. Back row, L-R: Margie Strickland Ward, Tommy Farmer.

Fresh Peach Cobbler

- *1/4 cup plus 2 tablespoons butter*
- *2 cups sugar (divided)*
- *3/4 cup all-purpose flour*
- *2 teaspoons baking powder with a pinch of salt*
- *3/4 cup milk*
- *2 cups sliced peaches*

Melt butter in a two-quart baking dish. Combine one cup sugar, flour, baking powder and salt. Add milk and stir until mixed. Pour batter over butter in baking dish but do not stir. Combine peaches and remaining one cup sugar. Spoon over the peaches. Do not stir. Bake at 350 degrees for one hour.—*Anne Seagraves, Clarke County, Georgia*

Celebrating Willie Belle's birthday. L-R: Siblings Mary Pettyjohn Norris Cape, Anne "Annie D" Pettyjohn Seagraves, Willie Belle Pettyjohn Strickland, Victor "Vic" Pettyjohn—From Margie Strickland Ward

Another Peach Cobbler

- *3/4 cup self-rising flour*
- *3/4 cup sugar*
- *3/4 cup sweet milk*
- *3/4 stick margarine*

Mix flour, sugar and sweet milk well. Melt three-fourth stick margarine in big baking dish or nine by thirteen by two-inch pan. Pour flour mixture over melted margarine. Do not stir.

- *1 quart (peeled) peaches, cut into pieces*
- *1/4 cup sugar*
- *1 teaspoon vanilla*

After peeling peaches, put sugar and vanilla over peaches and set aside. Add peaches over top of flour mixture in pan. Do not stir; spoon over. Bake at 325 degrees about thirty-five or forty minutes or until done.—*Anne Seagraves, Clarke County, Georgia*

Celebrating Anne "Annie D" Seagraves' 80th birthday at the Winterville depot, standing, L-R: Joe Gerling, Greg Seagraves, Donny Bailey Seagraves, Phillip Seagraves (at the door). Sitting at the table is William Gerling, Annie D's great-grandson.

Peach Cobbler

- *1 stick margarine*
- *1 cup self-rising flour*
- *1 cup white sugar*
- *3 cups sliced peaches (drain if using canned peaches)*
- *1 teaspoon lemon juice*
- *1 teaspoon vanilla extract*
- *1/2 teaspoon salt*

Preheat oven to 350 degrees. Mix margarine, flour and sugar using a knife into a coarse consistency, then set aside. Spray baking dish or pan with Baker's Joy. Combine peach slices (with extra sugar, to taste) with salt, lemon juice, vanilla extract. Pour mixture into a nine-by-thirteen-inch pan. Sprinkle flour mixture over the peaches. Bake at 350 degrees for forty minutes.—*Ann Seagraves, Madison County, Georgia*

Rev. Eugene "Gene" Pettyjohn delivering mail in downtown Athens, Georgia. Behind him is the Southern Mutual Building, now called "The Fred Building."

Fresh Peach Pie

- *5 cups (sliced) fresh peaches*
- *1 unbaked 9-inch pie shell*
- *1/3 cup margarine (melted)*
- *1 cup sugar*
- *1/3 cup all purpose flour*

- *1 egg*

Place peaches in pie shell. Combine margarine, sugar, flour and egg. Mix well and pour over peaches. Bake at 350 degrees for one hour and ten minutes.—*Anne Seagraves, Clarke County, Georgia*

The Seagraves family at a Pettyjohn family reunion in the backyard of the house on Boulevard in the 1970s. Front row, L-R: Annie D Pettyjohn Seagraves, Nelson "Petie" Seagraves, Mary Seagraves Fields. Back row, L-R: Billy Seagraves, Phillip Seagraves.

Key Lime Pie

- *5 egg yolks, beaten*
- *1 14-ounce can sweetened condensed milk*
- *1/2 cup key lime juice*
- *9-inch graham cracker crust pie shell (purchase ready-made)*

Preheat oven to 350 degrees. Combine egg yolks, sweetened condensed milk and lime juice. Mix well. Pour into unbaked graham cracker pie shell. Bake in preheated oven for fifteen minutes. Allow to cool completely. Top with Cool Whip and garnish with lime slices. *—Ann Seagraves, Madison County, Georgia*

Fresh Strawberry Pie

- *1 cup sugar*
- *1 cup water*
- *2 tablespoons cornstarch*
- *2 tablespoons margarine*
- *1/2 teaspoon red food coloring*
- *1 1/2 pints or 1 quart whole strawberries*
- *1 (9-inch) pie crust, baked and cooled*
- *Whipped cream for topping*

Combine sugar and cornstarch and cook with water, coloring and margarine. Stir and cook until mixture boils and thickens. Remove from heat and allow to cool completely. Fold in chilled berries. Pour into pie crust and chill. Serve with whipped cream or Cool Whip. *—Anne Seagraves, Clarke County, Georgia*

Lemon Pies

- *1 can Eagle Brand milk*
- *3 lemons (grated and juice, too)*
- *1 large carton Cool Whip*
- *1 package frozen coconut*
- *2 baked pie shells*

Add grated lemon rind and juice to the Eagle Brand milk. Add Cool Whip and coconut. Mix well. Put into baked pie shells.*—Anne Seagraves, Clarke County, Georgia*

Cousins swinging in the Seagraves' Georgia Drive house backyard: L-R: Phillip Seagraves, Margie Strickland Ward, Patricia Strickland Seabolt.

Magic Lemon Pie

Filling

- *1 crumb or baked (8-inch) pie shell*
- *1 can Eagle brand milk*
- *1/2 cup lemon juice or Real Lemon*
- *1 teaspoon grated lemon peel*
- *2 egg yolks (save whites)*

Mix milk, lemon juice, peel, and yolks in a mixing bowl until thickened. Fill pie shell.

Meringue

Beat egg whites until stiff and add one-half jar (seven ounces) marshmallow creme. Bake in slow 325-degree oven until top is brown, about fifteen minutes.—*Anne Seagraves, Clarke County, Georgia*

Pecan Pie

- *2 eggs*
- *2 tablespoons flour - Mix with eggs*
- *1 cup brown sugar*
- *1 cup syrup*
- *1 cup pecans*
- *1 teaspoon vanilla flavoring*

Mix all ingredients and pour into pie shell. Cook at 410 degrees for five minutes. Reduce heat to 350 degrees and cook twenty-five to thirty more minutes.—*Anne Seagraves, Clarke County, Georgia*

Pecan Pies (Makes 2)

- *1 box light brown or dark brown sugar*
- *4 eggs*
- *2 unbaked pie shells*
- *1/4 cup sweet milk*
- *3/4 stick margarine (melted)*
- *1 tablespoon flour*
- *Pinch of salt*
- *2 cups pecans (chopped)*

Mix all ingredients and pour into pie shells. Cook at 410 degrees for five minutes. Reduce heat to 350 degrees and cook twenty-five to thirty more minutes.—*Anne Seagraves, Clarke County, Georgia*

Lemon Cheese Filling

- *1 1/2 cups sugar*
- *4 1/2 tablespoons cornstarch*
- *1 teaspoon salt*
- *1 1/2 cups water*
- *3 tablespoons lemon rind*
- *2/3 cup lemon juice*
- *3 tablespoons butter*
- *6 egg yolks (beaten)*

Sift together sugar, salt and cornstarch in heavy pan. Blend thoroughly. Gradually add water, stirring constantly. Add lemon rind, juice and butter. Mix well. Place over low heat and let boil one minute, stirring constantly. Remove from heat. Gradually pour a little mixture over beaten egg yolks (beat constantly). Combine other egg mixture with hot mixture. Stir constantly. Cook about one minute until thick.—*Anne Seagraves, Clarke County, Georgia*

First All-Woman Jury Decides Case

Annie D served on the first-ever all-woman jury in Clarke County, Georgia. This *Athens Daily News* article about the all-woman jury was found in Annie D's papers.

The Daily News

First All-Woman Jury Decides Case

First All-Woman Jury in Clarke County Georgia Decides Case —Athens Banner Herald *newspaper clipping from Anne Seagraves' photo albums*

Twelve Clarke County women Monday became the first all-female jury to render a verdict in a criminal case in Clarke County City Court.

They may well have become a first also in the state of Georgia.

Judge Grady Pittard said he had never heard of an all-female jury in the county and believed it could be the first such in the state.

Clerk of Court King Crawford, who has been involved in court proceedings for over twenty years, said the local all-female jury was the first in the county. It was also a first for the attorneys who had never faced an entire jury of women.

They heard a case against Eugene Robinson, who had been accused of attempting to break into the Tau Epsilon Phi Fraternity House on Baxter Street.

The jury took just thirty-five minutes to return the verdict. They heard the charge from Judge Pittard and retired to the jury room at 4:40 p.m. after listening to testimony for more than two hours.

At 5:14, they returned to the courtroom, and Mrs. William R. Farber, foreperson of the all-woman jury, read the verdict.

City Solicitor Bill Gerard said he had never faced an all-female jury before.

Defense attorney Robert Peckham, director of the Athens Legal Aid and Defender Society, said he had never faced an all-female jury before.

"About the only difference is that you have to remember not to use 'ladies and gentlemen' when addressing the jury," the defense attorney added.

He and Mr. Gerard agreed the jury would be as good at deciding the guilt or innocence of a person as an all-male or a mixed jury.

Mr. Crawford explained that the city court judge draws at least forty names of qualified jurors for each term of court. For each case, a twelve-person jury is selected by the prosecutor and the defense attorney from twenty-four qualified jurors. The prosecutor can strike five names from the twenty-four and the defense attorney can strike seven.

Mr. Crawford said that of the twenty-four prospective jurors for the trial, thirteen were women. The two attorneys struck all the men from the list, leaving the first Athens all-female jury.

A check with local court officials and some state officers produced no knowledge of an all-female jury in the county or state.

Officials at the state Attorney General's office in Atlanta said they had never heard of such a jury before. Assistant Attorney General Matthew Robbins said, "Without extensive research, there is no way to say for sure," but he indicated it might be possible.

Dean Lindsey Cowan of the University of Georgia Law School said that he didn't think it was the first in the United States but knew of no previous all-female juries in Clarke County or Georgia.

Superior Court Judge James Barrow said, "I have never heard of such a case in Clarke County. As for Georgia, I wouldn't know."[2]

Chapter 22

Other Desserts

Cornelius Norris: Good Men Live on in Memories

Down a tree-lined street in Athens, Georgia, called Boulevard, behind a large frame house, inside a rustic workshop, there is a silence now more deafening than the sound of the loudest explosion. Power tools stand mute among the wood shavings while wood waits, raw and unformed, for expert hands that will never turn it into comfortable porch swings, whimsical animals, or sturdy cabinets.

Inside the vintage house, rooms filled with memories, both happy and sad, await the new widow's return from a visit with her son's family. Clothes hang in the closet, food spoils in the refrigerator, and cards of condolence pile up in the mailbox by the front door.

How does a widow ever return to such a place? How can she stand to walk among the rooms which still hold so much of her recently departed loved one's earthly essence — in the cushions and chairs, in the antique trunk and phonograph, in the pictures and cupboard drawers?

Cornelius Norris was a good man, a quiet shaper of wood and

lives. His friends were legion. His presence blessed his family. For many years he faithfully delivered the mail, pipe clenched between his teeth, blue uniform rumpled. This gentle, good-natured, curly-haired man brought bills and checks, good news and bad, to those who were fortunate enough to be on his route.

Cornelius and Mary Pettyjohn Norris in their house on Boulevard in Athens, Georgia

Cornelius and Mary Pettyjohn Norris—From Norris family albums

He led Boy Scout troops and was active in his church. He was a father to three boys, now grown men with families of their own, and he was the kind of husband to Mary that most women wish they could find and many never do.

"Neely," as some called him, was also a cancer patient during the last few months of his life. This man who retired to work in his shop with his hands was forced to give up one of those hands and the arm that held it. And like the opera singer who loses his voice or the champion runner who must give up a foot, Neely was devastated and bruised beyond repair by the treatment for his disease. The surgeon's scalpel cut so much deeper than the flesh.

A Cornelius Norris wooden medicine cabinet with a door made from a Dubl Handi washboard—Photo by Donny Bailey Seagraves

And so this fine man, who was very much alive just a few days ago, is gone. His tools are silent, his friends are grieving, and his family is still in shock over his passing.

Sooner or later, we will all face deafening silences and rooms filled with painful memories. Grief and suffering are just as much a part of life as the most breathtakingly beautiful sunrise and the joyful sight of a baby's first smile.

But just as the smiling baby will someday become the grieving widow or the older man, in time, deafening silences will be broken by happy sounds once again. And pleasant memories will crowd into rooms once filled with sadness.

Bottom row photos, L-R: Cornelius Norris, Mary Pettyjohn Norris (Cape), Ernest Strickland; David Norris; Norris house on Boulevard. Top row photos, L-R: Cornelius Norris; Norris brothers, David, Steve, Tommy celebrating their aunt Annie D's 80th birthday at the Winterville depot ; Mary Pettyjohn Norris and her husband Cornelius Norris.

And, like all good men, Cornelius Norris will live on. We will think of him while swinging on one of his handcrafted porch swings or clipping our favorite recipe card in the clothespin mouth of a whimsical wooden mule he once made for us.

And when we walk across a well-built by Uncle Neely porch

floor or open a medicine cabinet fashioned by his hands around a "Dubl Hands" washboard, we will remember Cornelius Norris and his talents and his undying love.[1]

Ambrosia

- *3 cups orange sections*
- *1 cup grated fresh coconut*
- *2 tablespoons sugar*
- *2 tablespoons powdered sugar*
- *1/2 cup whipping cream (whipped)*

Peel and cut orange sections (remove seeds). Combine oranges, coconut and sugar. Combine whipped cream and powdered sugar. Fold into fruit mixture. Refrigerate until time to serve.—*Anne Seagraves, Clarke County, Georgia*

Apple Fritters

- *1 cup flour*
- *1 teaspoon baking powder*
- *1 teaspoon powdered sugar*
- *1/4 teaspoon salt*
- *1/4 cup milk*
- *1 egg (beaten)*
- *2 apples (peeled and chopped)*
- *Vegetable oil*
- *Powdered sugar*

Combine dry ingredients in medium mixing bowl. Combine milk and egg and stir into dry ingredients. Stir in apples. Drop batter by tablespoons into deep, hot oil. Fry until brown, turning once. Drain on absorbent paper. Sprinkle with sugar.—*Anne Seagraves, Clarke County, Georgia*

Ann Shellnut Seagraves in her Madison County, Georgia kitchen—From Tristin Seagraves Johnson

Ann's Baked Apple Dumplings

- *4 medium-large apples*
- *2 cans Pillsbury Crescent Rolls*
- *1 12-ounce can of 7-Up or Sprite or Mountain Dew*
- *1 cup melted butter*
- *1 cup sugar*
- *1 teaspoon vanilla*

Preheat oven to 350 degrees. Mix melted butter with sugar and vanilla. Spray Pam into the nine-by-thirteen-inch Pyrex baking dish. Peel apples and slice down the side, creating four thick slices per apple. Spoon on top, pat onto each apple slice the melted butter, sugar and vanilla mixture, and sprinkle on cinnamon.

Wrap each coated apple slice with a crescent roll. Pat sugar and cinnamon on the outside of each crescent roll wrapped apple slices and gently place in the Pyrex baking dish. Carefully pour twelve-ounce 7-Up, Sprite or Mountain Dew into baking dish. Bake at 350 degrees for approximately forty minutes. Check for light golden brown color. Enjoy!—*Ann Seagraves, Madison County, Georgia*

Candy

- *1 12-ounce package semisweet chocolate chips*
- *1 cup chunky peanut butter or smooth*
- *4 cups miniature marshmallows*

Melt chocolate chips with peanut butter in saucepan over low heat, stirring until smooth. Fold in marshmallows. Pour into nine-inch square pan. Chill until firm. Cut into squares. Yields two dozen. —*Anne Seagraves, Clarke County, Georgia*

Coconut Dreams (Cherry)

- *20 marshmallows*
- *1 cup (drained) maraschino cherries*
- *1 tablespoon water*
- *1/2 cup nuts*
- *1 egg white*
- *1/4 teaspoon cream of tartar*
- *1 can (3 1/2 ounces) coconut*
- *3/4 cup sugar*
- *1 teaspoon vanilla*

Combine marshmallows and water in small saucepan. Cook over very low heat until marshmallows are melted. Beat egg white and cream of tartar until mixture forms peaks. Gradually beat in sugar.

Gradually beat in marshmallows and vanilla. Beat until mixture forms very stiff peaks. Fold in coconut, cherries and nuts. Turn into buttered eight-inch square pan. Chill overnight in refrigerator. To serve, cut into small squares.—*Anne Seagraves, Clarke County, Georgia*

Family members gathered in the dining room of Annie D's Winterville house. Front row, L-R: Annie D, Stacie Norris Brookshire (who passed away in 2018), Donny Bailey Seagraves, Stephanie Norris Compton, Marcia Fair Norris. Back row, L-R: Kevin Fields, Phillip Seagraves, Greg Seagraves, Steve Norris, Jen Seagraves and Mary Pettyjohn Norris Cape.

Something Different

- *1/2 cup sugar*
- *1 teaspoon cinnamon*

- *1/8 teaspoon almond extract*
- *1/4 cup melted butter*
- *1/2 teaspoon vanilla*
- *1 can buttermilk biscuits*
- *1 (3 ounce) package cream cheese (cut in cubes)*

Separate biscuits. Dip each cheese cube in butter mixture, then in sugar mixture. Place on biscuit. Fold dough over cheese, covering completely. Seal well, shaping into balls. Dip each filled biscuit in butter, then in sugar mixture. Place in ungreased muffin cup. Bake at 375 degrees for twelve to eighteen minutes.—*Anne Seagraves, Clarke County, Georgia*

Cranberry Jellies

- *1 (16-ounce) can jellied cranberry sauce*
- *2 (3-ounce) packs wild strawberry Jello*
- *1 cup finely chopped walnuts or pecans*

In a medium saucepan, combine the cranberry sauce and Jello. Cook and stir until mixture comes to a full rolling boil. Remove from heat and stir in nuts. Pour into a greased nine by five by three-inch loaf pan. Chill until firm, cut into one and one-fourth by three-fourth-inch pieces and roll in sugar, if desired. Store in the refrigerator. Makes forty pieces.—*Anne Seagraves, Clarke County, Georgia*

Divinity

- *2 2/3 cups sugar*
- *2/3 cup white Karo syrup*
- *2/3 cup water*
- *3 egg whites, beaten*
- *Nuts (chopped) optional*

Mix in a pot and cook until sugar and syrup spins a thread. Then beat until ready to drop onto waxed paper. Stir and add chopped nuts, if desired. Mix well and spoon onto wax paper.—*Anne Seagraves, Clarke County, Georgia*[2]

"Annie D's grandchildren's all-time favorite candy was divinity, which is believed to have originated in the United States during the early 1900s. The origins of the name are not clear. The most popular theory is simply that when it was first tasted, someone declared it "*Divine!*" and the name stuck. Annie D's divinity was certainly divine and we still think about it, especially at Christmas."

— Donny Bailey Seagraves

Georgia Depot Street to Georgia Drive

Mom (Annie D) didn't learn to drive until my older brother Billy got a car. Before that, she would call a cab and what usually happened was the driver would go downtown to the Georgia train depot to pick her up instead of coming to our house.

Intersection of Oconee Street and Georgia Drive—Photo by Donny Bailey Seagraves

Our street back then was called Georgia Depot Street because that area was the original location of the Georgia Railroad when it first came to Athens. The street was where the train tracks once were. The original train depot once was about where our house was. So that's what caused the confusion. Cab drivers expected to pick

Mom up at or near the depot in town because she lived on Georgia Depot Street.

In 1957, Mom decided to do something about her street name problem. She walked the neighborhood, getting neighbors to sign a petition to change the street's name to Georgia Drive.

An Oconee Street Methodist Church parking lot now occupies the space where the Seagraves house once stood on Georgia Drive.—Photo by Donny Bailey Seagraves

The local government accepted the petition and changed the street name from Georgia Depot Street to Georgia Drive.

After that, whenever Annie D called a cab, it arrived at our house on Georgia Drive instead of the train depot downtown. Mom loved that change.—Phillip Seagraves[3]

~

Mrs. Peeler's Date Candy

- *3 cups sugar*
- *1 teaspoon butter*
- *1 teaspoon vanilla*
- *1 cup milk*
- *1 pound dates*
- 1 cup chopped nuts

Cook sugar and milk until boiling. Add chopped dates and cook until it forms a soft ball in water. Add butter and vanilla, beat until stiff. Add nuts and beat again until really stiff. Roll in damp cloth and leave until dry, then slice.—*Mrs. Peeler, Clarke County, Georgia*

Luther "Luke" Pettyjohn and his Christmas Apples

ONE OF THE MOST refreshing stories emanating from the Christmas season is one about one of Uncle Sam's mail carriers and his little friends. Luther Pettyjohn who carries a mail

(Photo by REM Studio.)

MR. LUTHER PETTYJOHN

route in the South Milledge Avenue section must be very fond of children, certainly the little pre-school age tots on his route are very fond of him.

Meeting Mr. Pettyjohn as he delivers the mail each day is a big event for these youngsters and they have become fast good friends. Mr. Pettyjohn wanted to remember his little friends at Christmas so he bought a box of big red apples and gave one to each pre-school age small fry. Seems the apples and the children came out even, of the box of 100 apples there were only three left. The children were thrilled to pieces to get the big red apple from Mr. Pettyjohn. And we think it was a charming gesture.

Mr. and Mrs. Pettyjohn and their 13-year old daughter, Carol live at 335 Southview Drive. He has been in the Post Office's employment ten years.

An undated newspaper article about Luther "Luke" Pettyjohn, younger brother of Anne "Annie D" Pettyjohn Seagraves.

Date Fingers

- *1 1/2 sticks margarine*
- *2 cups sugar*
- *2 eggs, beaten*
- *1/2 pound package dates, chopped*
- *1 1/2 cups Rice Krispies*
- *1 cup nuts*
- *2 teaspoons vanilla*
- *1 box finely grated coconut*

Melt margarine. Add eggs, sugar and dates. Cook ten minutes after it comes to a boil. Keep stirring so dates won't stick. Cook on low heat and add vanilla, nuts, and Rice Krispies. When cool, roll in coconut. *—Anne Seagraves, Clarke County, Georgia*

Agnes' Fudge

- *2/3 cup evaporated milk*
- *1 and 2/3 cup sugar*
- *1/2 teaspoon salt*
- *1 1/2 cups (16 medium diced marshmallows)*
- *1 and 1/2 cups or 1 6-ounce package chocolate chips*
- *1 teaspoon vanilla*
- *1/2 cup chopped nuts*

Mix evaporated milk, sugar, salt in saucepan over low heat. Heat to boiling and cook five minutes, stirring constantly. Remove from heat and add marshmallows, chocolate chips, vanilla and chopped nuts.

Stir one to two minutes until marshmallows melt. Pour into buttered nine-inch pan. Cool and cut into squares.*—Agnes Pettyjohn Russell, Whitfield County, Georgia*

Phillip Seagraves with his sister Mary Seagraves Fields making homemade ice cream July 8, 1996 in the Seagraves' house in Winterville.—Photo by Donny Bailey Seagraves

Ice Cream in Crank Freezer

- *4 eggs*
- *2 cans evaporated milk (large)*
- *2 cans water in cans (large)*
- *3 cans whole milk*
- *1/2 teaspoon salt*
- *3 cups chopped fruit (peaches or strawberries)*
- *1 3/4 cups sugar*
- *1 teaspoon vanilla*
- *1/4 teaspoon almond flavoring*

Beat eggs, add sugar and heat until stiff. Add canned milk, salt, vanilla and about two cups milk. Pour into freezing can, finishing filling to fill line with rest of milk. Freeze as you would in any hand-turned freezer or electric ice cream freezer.—*Anne Seagraves, Clarke County, Georgia*

"One of our favorite long-ago treats was homemade ice cream. Back in the day, we used a hand-cranked ice cream freezer. Mom would mix up a batch of ice cream using one of the recipes in this chapter. Later on, she used an electric ice cream freezer, and that made it a lot easier to make homemade ice cream."

— Phillip Seagraves

Peach Ice Cream

- *6-8 fresh peaches*
- *2 cups sugar*
- *2 - 13-ounce cans of Carnation evaporated milk*
- *1 - 12-ounce jar apricot nectar*

Peel peaches and set aside. Mix all ingredients, except peaches, and stir until sugar is dissolved. Squeeze in peeled peaches. Churn (in an old-fashioned ice cream freezer) until frozen. Makes one gallon. —*Anne Seagraves, Clarke County, Georgia*

Short on Sherbet

Pour contents of a thirty-ounce can of cling peaches into blender and stir until liquid. Add one tablespoon of lemon juice and freeze. Stir occasionally if you think of it.—*Anne Seagraves, Clarke County, GA*

Pettyjohn family members on the steps of the Boulevard homeplace. Front row, L-R: Agnes Pettyjohn Russell holding dog, Mary Seagraves Fields and behind her Billy Seagraves. Back row, L-R: David Norris, Mary Pettyjohn Norris Cape, Annie D Pettyjohn Seagraves

Sinful Dessert

- *1 1/2 cups graham cracker crumbs*
- *1/4 cup sugar*
- *1/3 cup melted butter or margarine*
- *1 package (8 ounces) cream cheese, softened*
- *2 tablespoons milk*
- *1 8-ounce container of Cool Whip, thawed*
- *2 packs (4-ounce size) Jello chocolate instant pudding*
- *3 1/2 cups cold milk*

Combine cracker crumbs, sugar and melted butter. Press firmly into bottom of thirteen by nine-inch pan. Beat cream cheese with sugar and two tablespoons milk until smooth. Fold in half the Cool Whip. Spread over crust. Using the cold milk, prepare pudding as directed on package. Pour over cream cheese layer. Chill several hours or overnight. Spread remaining Cool Whip over pudding. Garnish with grated chocolate or topping of chopped nuts, if desired. Serves twelve to fifteen.—*Anne Seagraves, Clarke County, Georgia*

Smooth Orange Dessert

- 1 (10 1/2 ounce) package miniature marshmallows
- 2 cups orange juice
- Whipped topping
- Orange sections

Combine marshmallows and orange juice in top of double boiler. Stir over medium heat until smooth, but do not cook. Spoon into compotes and chill until ready to serve. Garnish with toppings and orange sections. Serves six.—*Anne Seagraves, Clarke County, Georgia*

The 215 Georgia Drive House

Our house at 215 Georgia Drive was very close to where the original Athens train depot was once located. When I was a little boy, I enjoyed playing out in the backyard under a giant tree that's no longer there. Daddy (Petie Seagraves) used to say that back when the train tracks and depot were there, train engineers sat in the shade of that tree when they took breaks.

Daddy also said our Georgia Drive house was moved to the lot on Georgia Depot Street (later renamed Georgia Drive). It's my understanding that the houses at 205 and 215 Georgia Drive were moved to Georgia Depot Street about 1948 by Clifford Denny, who was a local electrician and builder and our neighbor. Daddy told me those houses were once on lots across from Chicopee Mill.

I have a copy of a 1926 Sanborn map that shows the houses originally were on Pine Street. A parking lot is there now, where the houses once were located. The lot where our former house on Georgia Drive stood is also now a parking lot. The house was moved across town a couple of years ago.—Phillip Seagraves

The Seagraves 215 Georgia Drive house. Bottom photos, L-R: The Georgia Drive house was moved across town and, at the time this book was written, was a rental house, connected to another rental house; Annie D in her Georgia Drive house kitchen, back in the day; the Georgia Drive house kitchen as it looked before the house was moved. Top row photos, L-R: Phillip Seagraves in the yard of the Georgia Drive house about 1953 or 1954; Nelson "Petie" and Annie D Seagraves with son Phillip on the front porch; our favorite photo of the Georgia Drive house.

Chapter 23

Other Recipes

For a Pretty Complexion

Buy a few ounces of hydrophilic petrolatum (petroleum jelly) from a druggist. In the evening, first soak the face for a few minutes with a warm towel. Pat dry and apply the petrolatum. Repeat every night.—*Anne Seagraves, Clarke County, Georgia*

Chili Sauce

- *1/2 gallon vinegar - maybe less*
- *7 1/2 pounds sugar (15 cups)*
- *5 to 6 pods green hot pepper*
- *1 gallon (16 cups) tomatoes — measured after blending with green hot pepper (9 - 10 large tomatoes)*

Bring sugar and vinegar to a boil. Pour tomatoes and peppers in and cook for two and one-third to three hours on medium heat until mixture thickens and changes (take a tablespoon of mixture and cool in fridge. If it thickens, it is ready.) Pour in sterilized pint jars and seal. Yield: Nine pints. Good on beans and peas.—*Mrs. James Roy Seagraves, Sr. (Dessie Mae), Madison County, Georgia*[1]

Pettyjohn siblings with their mother, Ethel. Front row, L-R: Mary Pettyjohn Norris Cape, Ethel Pettyjohn. Back row, L-R: Vic Pettyjohn, Willie Belle Pettyjohn Strickland, Agnes Pettyjohn Russell, Gene Pettyjohn, Luke Pettyjohn, Anne "Annie D" Pettyjohn Seagraves.

Dill Dandies - 3 Quarts

- *24 large cucumbers (or what you have to fill three-quart jars)*
- *Cold water*
- *Canning jars*
- *1/8 teaspoon alum*

- *1 clove of garlic*
- *2 heads dill*

Wash twenty-four large cucumbers, or what you have to fill three-quart jars. Cover with cold water. Let stand overnight. Pack in jars. Add to each jar: one eighth teaspoon alum, one clove of garlic, two heads dill.

Combine and bring to boil:

- *2 cups cider vinegar*
- *1/2 cup coarse salt*
- *6 cups water*

Seal and store six weeks.—*Anne Seagraves, Clarke County, Georgia*

Pettyjohn descendants, L-R: Kelli Ward, Steve Norris, Margie Strickland Ward, David Norris and his wife Gaynelle, Sharon Strickland Farmer, Tommy Norris, Mary Seagraves Fields, Phillip Seagraves—Photo by Donny Bailey Seagraves

Energy Booster

Are you planning to clean house for two hours? One glass of milk will provide enough energy for doing the two hours of housework.—*Anne Seagraves, Clarke County, Georgia*

Home Brewed Vanilla Extract

- *2 cups vodka*
- *5 vanilla beans cut into 1-inch pieces*

Combine vodka and beans in a jar with a tight-fitting lid. Cover the jar and let stand six to eight weeks. The vodka mixture will turn amber-colored after a day or two. After one-half the vanilla is used, add more vodka to cover the beans. The flavor in the beans is gone when the vodka no longer turns to a dark color. Yields two cups - sixteen ounces.—*Anne Seagraves, Clarke County, Georgia*

Homemade Cottage Cheese

- *1/2 gallon clabbered milk*
- *Melted butter or sweet cream*
- *1 tablespoon to the quart (salt to taste)*

Place utensil with ingredients in a pan of hot water and heat until the curd separates (don't let it boil). When the mixture gets too hot, it becomes tough. You can wait until mixture finishes heating before working in the salt and cream.—*Anne Seagraves, Clarke County, Georgia*

L-R: June Pettyjohn Blackwell, her mother Floy Jordan Pettyjohn, and her brother Michael "Mike" Pettyjohn. Not pictured is Vic Pettyjohn, who was June and Mike's dad and Floy's husband.— From Norris family albums

Homemade Sweetened Condensed Milk

- *1 cup instant nonfat dry milk powder*
- *2/3 cup sugar*
- *1/3 cup boiling water*
- *3 tablespoons melted butter*

Combine all ingredients in blender and process until smooth. Store in refrigerator until ready to use. Makes one and three-fourth cups. —*Anne Seagraves, Clarke County, Georgia*

Homemade Vanilla Flavoring

- *1 cup brandy*
- *2 vanilla beans, cut into 1-inch pieces*

Combine brandy and vanilla beans in a jar with a tight-fitting lid. Cover and let stand three months, shaking three times a week. Yields one cup.—*Anne Seagraves, Clarke County, Georgia*

Petie and Annie D Seagraves enjoying a vacation at Dudley Creek Motel in Gatlinburg, Tennessee.

Pear Honey

- *8 ripe pears, peeled, quartered and pared*
- *4 cups sugar*
- *1 15 l/2-ounce can crushed pineapple*

Combine pears and sugar in a heavy skillet or saucepan and bring the mixture to a boil, frequently stirring until sugar dissolves. Reduce heat and simmer forty-five minutes. Add drained pineapple and cook five minutes longer. Annie D included a note on this recipe that said it was good as a filling for fried pies.—*Sybil Crowe, Clarke County, Georgia*

Pear Relish

- *1-peck pears*
- *5 medium size onions*
- *6 bell peppers (3 red and 3 green), seeded*
- *2 pounds sugar*
- *1 tablespoon salt*
- *1 tablespoon mixed spices*
- *1 tablespoon of turmeric (for color)*
- *3 cups vinegar*

Remove peelings on pears. Seed peppers. Peel onions. Run pears, onions and peppers through meat chopper and add other ingredients. Cook for thirty minutes after it begins to boil. Put in jars and seal. —*Anne Seagraves, Clarke County, Georgia*

Pepper Jelly

- *1 cup bell peppers*
- *1/2 cup hot peppers*
- *5 cups vinegar*
- *1 bottle Certo*

Grind peppers. Add vinegar and sugar. Boil one and one-half minutes. Remove from heat. Add Certo and stir real good for two minutes. Put in jars or seal in jelly glasses with paraffin wax. Good with crackers and cream cheese.—*Anne Seagraves, Clarke County, Georgia*

Russian Tea

- 1 large can pineapple juice
- 1 large can orange juice
- 4 lemons (juice squeezed)
- 4 sticks cinnamon

Make tea as usual (strain). Add all together.—*Anne Seagraves, Clarke County, Georgia*

Ernest and Willie Belle Pettyjohn Strickland with their daughter Sharon Strickland Farmer—From Norris family albums

Self Rising Flour Made From Plain Flour

- *10 pounds of plain flour*
- *1 cup baking powder*
- *5 teaspoons soda*

- *5 tablespoons salt*

Mix well. Can make a half recipe of this using five pounds of plain flour, one-half cup baking powder, two and one-half tablespoons salt and two and one-half teaspoons soda.—*Anne Seagraves, Clarke County, Georgia*

Nelson "Petie" and Anne "Annie D" Seagraves cuddling in their Georgia Drive house living room.

Recipe for a Happy Marriage

- *1 cup consideration*
- *1 cup courtesy*
- *2 cups flattery, carefully concealed*
- *2 cups human kindness*
- *1-gallon faith in God and in each other*

- *2 cups praise*
- *1 small pinch of in-laws*
- *1 reasonable budget*
- *A generous dash of cooperation*
- *3 teaspoons pure extract of "I'm Sorry"*
- *1 cup contentment*
- *1 cup confidence and encouragement*
- *2 (or 3) children*
- *1 large or several hobbies*
- *1 cup blindness to other's faults*

Flavor with frequent portions of recreation and a dash of happy memories. Stir well and remove any specks of jealousy, temper or criticism. Sweeten with generous portions of love. Keep warm with a steady flame of devotion. Never serve with a cold shoulder or a hot tongue.

Amen,

Annie D Seagraves, Clarke County, Georgia

Afterword

Exa Annie Derrell "Annie D" Pettyjohn Seagraves and Nelson Hardy "Petie" Seagraves lived most of their lives together in Athens, Georgia. They spent many of those years in their house on Georgia Drive, in the Carr's Hill neighborhood, near Sanford Stadium.

Anne "Annie D" Pettyjohn Seagraves and Nelson Hardy "Petie" Seagraves at the door of their house on Georgia Drive one long ago Christmas

Pete often called the cozy white house his "little rabbit box." It might not be much, he used to say, but it's mine. Indeed, after serving as an Army medic in Germany during WWII, moving away from Athens twice and even after buying and living in a much newer and more spacious house in a popular Athens subdivision, Pete always insisted on returning to the house on Georgia Drive.

Annie D visiting Petie at the Veteran's Administration hospital in Augusta, Georgia, where he spent his last days after suffering several strokes.

Well, great things can happen in small houses. Some of us still smell the biscuits baking in the cozy Georgia Drive house kitchen. Meals from years ago are tasted in our dreams. Penny poker games that weren't about accumulating pennies, but were times to gather and have fun with family, still go on in our minds. And we will never forget those Christmas celebrations full of seemingly endless cakes, divinity, and family. There were gifts, too, but they weren't what our time together was all about.

Overall, Annie D and Petie Seagraves lived a good life and shared it all with those they loved.

Now you have their recipes. Cook Anne's favorite pound cake.

Make a batch of Seagraves' bar-b-que sauce the way Fid and Len did so long ago. Find pennies for a kitchen table poker game, if you can.

It's your turn. As Petie used to say, "Get on with it!"

Jo Seagraves, Nelson "Petie" and Anne "Annie D" Seagraves in the Georgia Drive house kitchen—From Sandy Seagraves

Selected Bibliography

This book began as a simple collection of recipes from Anne "Annie D" Pettyjohn Seagraves. Along the way, we added photos, family history, memories, recipes from others and more. This selected bibliography lists many of the most important sources of information in this book, along with other books and websites that may interest Seagraves, Pettyjohns and others.

Addall, Used Books and Out-of-Print Book Finder. https://www.addall.com/used.

Arnold, Patsy Hawkins and Easom, Maxine Pinson. *Across The River: The People, Places, and Culture of East Athens*. Self-published, 2019.

Athens Banner-Herald, Athens Daily News, Classic Scene Sunday Magazine. Several articles and newspaper columns, some dates unknown.

Athens-Clarke County website. http://accgov.com.

Athens Convention & Visitors Bureau. *Athens of Old*. The publication date is unknown.

Athens, Georgia Historical Timeline. https://www.accgov.com/115/Historical-Timeline.

Atlanta Constitution. Cooking with Fatback, Good Will: Athens Cafe Has Recipe for Loyalty by Kent Hannon, July 18, 1984.

Boulevard Historic District website. https://www.boulevardathens.com/neighborhood-history.com.

Chenille Bedspread History. https://www.georgiaencyclopedia.org/articles/arts-culture/chenille-bedspreads.

City of Athens, Georgia Mayor and Council. *Athens, Georgia: Home of the University of Georgia 1801 - 1951*.

Chamberlain, Era Jane Pettyjohn and Pettyjohn, Clive Abraham. *Something of the Pettijohn (Pettyjohn) Family With Particular Reference to the Descendants of James Pettyjohn of Hungar's Parish, Northampton County, Virginia*. Privately printed, 1948. Available to read at http://www.pettyjohn.net.

Crockford-Pigeon Mountain website. https://georgiawildlife.com/crockford-pigeon-mountain-wma.

Doster, Gary L. *Athens Streets and Neighborhoods*. Deeds Publishing, 2021.

Family Search website. http://familysearch.org.

Find a Grave website. http://www.findagrave.com.

Hull, Augustus Longstreet. *Annals of Athens, Georgia 1801 - 1901 with an Introduc-*

tory Sketch by Dr. Henry Hull. Available in a free digital version at http://books.google.com.

Madison County GA website. http://madisoncountyga.us.

Marshall, Charlotte Thomas, editor. *The Tangible Past in Athens, Georgia.* Self-published and bound by Thompson-Shore, Dexter, MI, 2014.

Morris, Sylvanus, 1855-1929. *Strolls about Athens during the early seventies / Sylvanus Morris.* University of Georgia Libraries. 1912, http://dlg.galileo.usg.edu/georgiabooks/do-pdf:gb0504

My Heritage website. http://myheritage.com.

National Center for Home Food Preservation. https://nchfp.uga.edu/#gsc.tab=0.

Pettijohn Family website. http://pettijohn.net.

Pigeon Mountain (*Georgia website*). http:en.m.wikipedia.org/wiki/Pigeon_Mountain.

The Police Review. Publisher unknown. 1926.

Reap, James K. *Athens: A Pictorial History.* The Donning Company/Publishers, 1985.

Sartain, James Alfred. *History of Walker County Georgia Volume 1.* A.J. Showalter Company, Dalton, Ga. 1932. Available online: https://books.google.com.

Seagraves Family in America website. http://theseagravesfamilyinamerica.com.

Seagraves, Pettyjohn and related family history. https://ancestry.com.

Tate, William. *Strolls Around Athens.* The Observer Press, 1975.

Vintage Chenille Bedspreads: A Brief History. https://cottagedivine.com/history-of-vintage-chenille-bedspreads/.

Walker, Myra C. Manley Watkins. *Segraves/Seagraves and Related Families of North Georgia.* Self-published, 1993.

Some books listed in this selected bibliography are long out of print. To locate a copy, first look in a library, either in person or on the library website. If you don't find a copy there, search the website https://www.addall.com/used. This search engine searches book sites across the internet, including Amazon.com, Alibris.com and many others.

Notes

2. Appetizers

1. This information on the origins of the Segraves/Seagraves surname is from Ances try.com.
2. This information on another possible origin of the Segraves/Seagraves surname is from Ancestry.com.
3. The information about Seagraves in America came from the website: https://theseagravesfamilyinamerica.com. There is much more information there on the Segraves/Seagraves family.
4. When one of Annie D's recipes calls for "sweet" milk or milk (sweet), this means use whole milk.

3. Early Seagraves Family History

1. This excerpt about Segraves/Seagraves family history is from Myra C. Manley Watkins Walker's book, *Segraves/Seagraves and Related Families of Northeast Georgia*. This book is long out of print. Information in this chapter came from a draft of the manuscript found in the papers of Rebecca Seagraves Baugh.

4. Hardy Seagraves: From Madison County to Athens, Georgia

1. Infant mortality rate when Hardy and Andy Seagraves were born is estimated using online information sources, including https://www.statista.com.
2. Family history information here and in the rest of this chapter and other parts of this book is from family legend and stories, ancestry.com, and the book *Segraves/Seagraves and Related Families of Northeast Georgia*, by Myra C. Manley Watkins Walker.
3. Some of the information about Typhoid Fever is from the article, "When Typhoid Was Dreaded" by Thomas V. DiBacco, published January 25, 1994 in *The Washington Post*. Other information on Typhoid Fever is from family legend.
4. Information about family history is from family legend and stories and Ances try.com.
5. Family history information is from Ancestry.com. Athens, Clarke County, Georgia information on population is estimated from an article "Athens" on the website: https://georgiaencyclopedia.org.
6. Information about the wall on the Carr family property is from the book *Strolls About Athens During the Early Seventies* by Sylvanus Morris

7. See the Selected Bibliography for sources of the Athens history information.
8. *Athens Weekly Banner*

8. Seagraves Mill

1. A copy of "The History of Seagraves Mill" by an unknown author was given to me more than 30 years ago by Ann Shellnut Seagraves. Some other information that helped clarify information in the mill history was shared by John and Todd Seagraves, sons of Weyman Seagraves. Tristin Seagraves Johnson also helped with this information and some information came from Wikipedia.
2. The article "The History of Seagraves Mill" was written in 1954 by an unknown author. A copy of this article was given to Donny Bailey Seagraves by Ann Shellnut Seagraves, widow of Weyman Seagraves, the last Seagraves to own Seagraves Mill. Weyman was a son of Arthur Ford Seagraves who was a son of Josiah Milsey Seagraves, the first Seagraves to own Seagraves Mill.

9. Main Dishes

1. The tradition of quail hunting goes back to the antebellum South and is as Southern as barbecue, college football and sweet tea. Information about quail in this book is from family legend, along with an article entitled, "Why Southern Fried Quail is Just as Traditional as Chicken," from the website: www.southernkitchen.com.
2. Information on chicken mull is from family legend and wikipedia.com. From wikipedia: "Chicken mull is a type of stew consisting of parboiled whole chicken in a cream or milk based broth, butter and it's seasoned with salt, pepper and other ingredients. Traditionally, the stew is served in the late fall or winter months. In northern Georgia, this part of the year is often referred to as "mull season." Often the term "chicken stew" or "chicken mull" refers to an event or gathering where the dish is served." Annie D crumbled up soda crackers and put those into her chicken mull, along with ketchup. Some cooks serve chicken mull with crackers and ketchup on the side.
3. Sources: "Cooking with Fatback, Good Will: Athens Cafe Has Recipe for Loyalty" by Kent Hannon, published in *The Atlanta Constitution* (Atlanta, Georgia), July 18, 1984 plus Mark Edward Hansford Obituary, February 11, 2015, *Athens Banner-Herald* and family stories and information.

10. Meats, Fish, Seafood

1. This article, written by Donny Bailey Seagraves, was first published on the *Athens Daily News* editorial page, circa late 1980s - early 1990s.

11. Barbecue

1. Some of the information in this article, written by Donny Bailey Seagraves, originally appeared in an earlier piece, also written by her and published in the *Athens Banner-Herald/The Daily News Classic Scene Sunday Magazine*, Sunday, August 2, 1987.
2. Some information in this chapter came from Judd Farr, Jr.'s obituary and family memories.

12. Papa Bob and His Children

1. Information about the Seagraves farm on Gaines School Road is from family memories and legend.
2. Information on the nickname Gobby is from family legend and the website names.org.
3. Some information about Harvey Lee "Bob" Seagraves and his children is from their obituaries and family history, stories and legend.

13. Public Safety

1. This quote and some other information is from an article entitled, "Charles E. Seagraves, Chief of Detectives," *The Police Review* (National Issue), 5, no. 3, March 1926, 203. Several pages from this magazine were found in Annie D Seagraves' papers.
2. Information about Hard Charlie's nickname came from family legend and a 1980s interview by Donny Bailey Seagraves with Bessie Seagraves Kemp, Charles Emory "Hard Charlie" Seagraves' daughter.

14. Side Dishes

1. Several recipes in this book tell the reader to "put in jars and seal." If you are unfamiliar with how to can and preserve food, be sure to read a book on the subject or visit a website such as National Center for Home Food Preservation: https://nchfp.uga.edu, where you'll find information on how to can, freeze, dry, cure & smoke, ferment, pickle, make jam and jelly and store food.
2. Some information in this article is from Wikipedia and the OK Cafe website.

15. Cakes

1. This article by Donny Bailey Seagraves was published many years ago in the *Athens Banner-Herald, The Athens Daily News Classic Scene Sunday Magazine.*

2. Source: *The Daily News*, from a Donny Bailey Seagraves column circa 1980s - 1990s

17. Pettyjohn Family History

1. This Pettyjohn family history article was researched and written by Luther "Luke" Pettyjohn and his wife Mabel Farr Pettyjohn. Luke and Mabel researched and wrote this article without the use of online sources, which were not available at the time. Luke's brother Rev. Eugene "Gene" Pettyjohn researched Pettyjohn family history and contributed some information and photos.

18. The Pettyjohns Move to Athens, Georgia

1. Information on Dalton, Georgia, Dalton's textile mills and bedspread industry, came from several websites, including HMdb.org - Dalton in Whitfield County, Georgia — The American South (South Atlantic): Our Textile Legacy, westgatex tiletrail.com and Cottagedevine.com, History of Chenille.
2. Some information about Athens, Georgia history, including approximate 1933 population, is from Wikipedia.
3. Information for the Boulevard neighborhood came from several different sources, including the Historic Boulevard Neighborhood Georgia website: www.boulevar dathens.com and the book, *Athens, A Pictorial History* by James K. Reap, The Donning Company, Publishers, Norfolk, Virginia, 1985.

20. Cookies

1. This article by Donny Seagraves originally appeared in the *Athens Daily News*, circa 1980s-1990s.
2. This article by Donny Bailey Seagraves appeared in the *Athens Daily News*, Wednesday morning, January 20, 1988.

21. Pies

1. Some information about Ruby Williams is from her obituary, published November 4, 2007, in the *Tampa Bay Times*. Ruby lived in Chattanooga, Tennessee and St. Petersburg, Florida.
2. This article originally appeared in the *Athens Daily News*, Northeast Georgia's Morning Newspaper, Volume 5 - Number 39, Athens, Georgia 30601, Tuesday Morning, February 25, 1969. This clipping was found in Annie D's papers.

22. Other Desserts

1. This column by Donny Bailey Seagraves appeared in the Wednesday, May 18, 1988 edition of the *Athens Daily News*. Cornelius Norris' widow, Mary Pettyjohn Norris Cape, was Annie D's younger sister.
2. Divinity, a favorite of Annie's D's grandchildren and other family members, is believed to have originated in the U.S. during the early 1900s. The origins of the name of this popular "Southern candy" are not clear. But the most popular theory is simply that when first tasted, someone a long time ago declared it to be "Divine!" The name stuck and today divinity recipes can be found in many cookbooks. In Annie D's granddaughter Jen Seagraves memories, she recalls that sometimes her grandmother's divinity would flop. Humidity during preparation can affect the quality of divinity. For a successful batch of divinity, the humidity must be low enough (less than 50%) for the candy to dry properly. From the website: https://en.m.wikipedia.org/wiki/Divinity_
3. This memory came from Annie D's son Phillip Seagraves. The year when Annie D walked the neighborhood and got neighbors on Georgia Depot Street to sign the petition to change the street name to Georgia Drive came from Gary L. Doster's book: *Athens Streets and Neighborhoods*. Deeds Publishing, 2021. Phillip remembered everything but the year of the petition.

23. Other Recipes

1. Several recipes in this book tell the reader to "put in jars and seal." If you are unfamiliar with how to can and preserve food, be sure to read a book on the subject or visit a website such as National Center for Home Food Preservation: https://nchfp.uga.edu, where you'll find information on how to can, freeze, dry, cure & smoke, ferment, pickle, make jam and jelly and store food.

Disclaimer

The information in this book came from various sources, including recipes, newspaper clippings and other memorabilia left for us by Anne "Annie D" Pettyjohn Seagraves. We have tried to make this book as accurate as possible and apologize for any errors you may find. Please email donnyseagraves@gmail.com with corrections and/or information you feel might be helpful in future editions.

About the Author

Donny Bailey Seagraves is an American author living in Athens, Georgia, USA. She is a native of Athens and has been a freelance newspaper columnist and magazine article writer for many years. Donny also writes fiction and nonfiction for adults and children. Her children's middle-grade novel, *Gone From These Woods,* was published by Penguin Random House. When not writing, Donny works in her business, Junebug Books and Collectibles, which she founded in 1998. For more information, visit her website: https://donnyseagraves.com.

facebook.com/donnybaileyseagraves

twitter.com/donnyseagraves

instagram.com/donnybaileyseagraves

Also by Donny Bailey Seagraves

Gone From These Woods

Gone From These Woods by Donny Bailey Seagraves is a children's middle-grade and YA novel set in rural North Georgia near Athens and published by Penguin Random House.

For more information, visit https://donnyseagraves.com.

Newsletter Sign Up

I hope you enjoyed reading *Cooking With Annie D: Southern Recipes Seasoned With Seagraves and Pettyjohn Family History*.

Please visit my website: https://donnyseagraves.com to sign up for my newsletter, read more about my books and see more Seagraves and Pettyjohn family photos. And don't forget to leave positive reviews for *Cooking With Annie D* online.

Thanks!

— Donny Bailey Seagraves

Made in the USA
Columbia, SC
03 December 2022